Old Gray Cemetery
~ in ~
Knoxville

OLD GRAY CEMETERY
~ IN ~
KNOXVILLE

JUDY LOEST

THE
History
PRESS

Published by The History Press
Charleston, SC
www.historypress.com

Front cover: photo by Judy Loest.
Back cover: photo by Judy Loest.

First published 2023

Manufactured in the United States

ISBN 9781467154826

Library of Congress Control Number: 2023934822

Notice: The information in this book is true and complete to the best of our knowledge. It is offered without guarantee on the part of the author or The History Press. The author and The History Press disclaim all liability in connection with the use of this book.

Alexine "Alix" Frincke Dempster (1939–2017),
Old Gray Executive Director (1986–2017)

CONTENTS

ACKNOWLEDGEMENTS

I would like to thank Steve Cotham and Danette Welch, McClung Collection, East Tennessee Historical Society; Jack Neely and Paul James, Knoxville History Project; Laura Still, Knoxville Walking Tours; Ellen Rochelle, Old Gray executive director, whose professional computer skills were invaluable; Knoxville Public Library System for its online genealogy resources and extra home access during COVID; Old Gray Board of Trustees, past and present, for preservation, maintenance and enhancement of Old Gray through the decades; and, most especially, Flossie McNabb, Old Gray trustee and secretary and the proprietor of Union Avenue Books, without whose advice, encouragement and friendship this book would not have been possible.

INTRODUCTION

If you are a lover of old cemeteries, especially the cemeteries that grew out of the rural or garden cemetery movement of the nineteenth century, you will find few more beautiful than Old Gray Cemetery in Knoxville, Tennessee. And even if you're not a cemetery enthusiast (otherwise known as a taphophile, grave hunter, or necro tourist), you will find much to admire and enjoy in this historic, park-like sanctuary.

Although Old Gray does not reflect population diversity, it does open a window into the eastern European immigrant experience. The people buried in Old Gray during its early decades experienced pivotal points in both European and American southern history. Some of them played important roles in bringing commercial and urban development to East Tennessee, and some led obscure but interesting lives. We chose a few of them at random. Since women are often invisible in early documented history, we also tried to amplify some of these forgotten lives. Although many individuals were successful in their occupations, history makes clear that we are not self-made creatures; we are social animals who depend on personal connections and circumstances to shape our paths. We hope these stories reconnect readers to their neighbors, their community, their city and, perhaps, the larger world.

We hope, too, that the book serves as a sort of field guide for visitors who are interested in subjects that can be explored here: genealogy, local history, cemetery symbolism and iconography, funerary architecture and materials and botany and arboriculture. (Old Gray was certified as a Level I Arboretum by the Tennessee Urban Forestry Council in 2013.)

One doesn't have to be a cemetery enthusiast to enjoy walking in Old Gray. Although a cemetery is naturally a sacred place of remembrance, inspiration and solace, it can also be a place to escape the noise and stress of our warp-speed modern culture and to find the necessary space for reflection and meditation. A cemetery, as opposed to a typical urban park, which is full of activity and noise, is a liminal space—from the Latin *limen* ("threshold")—akin to libraries, museums and old forests, to name a few. It is a crossroads of contradictory or ambivalent principles (life and death, the past and eternity, order and the unknown, despair and hope), a transitional space of heightened intensity. French philosopher and historian Michel Foucault created a term for these places, *heterotopias*, spaces that he claimed elicited "profound spatio-temporal disruption," an "absolute break with traditional time." It is in such places that the imagination is freed from the rigid regularity of daily schedules and calendars.

Whatever your reasons for visiting Old Gray, we hope that you find here a momentary break from the ten thousand things that clamor for your attention.

PART I

BACKGROUND

1

HISTORY OF OLD GRAY CEMETERY

By the 1840s, the garden cemetery movement, driven largely by the fame of Paris's Père Lachaise Cemetery, had gained popularity in France, England and the United States. Urban planners began building larger, more elaborate cemeteries in their respective cities' outskirts and suburbs. Public-health concerns also motivated leaders to locate cemeteries away from urban centers. The first and oldest burial ground in Knoxville is First Presbyterian Church Graveyard, near the center of town, founded in 1792. Many residents incorrectly believed that the graveyard had caused a deadly cholera epidemic in 1838. The 1836–38 diary of Nancy Dickinson Estabrook mentions the cholera epidemic that struck Knoxville that year, "listing many of its victims by name and calculating that 'upwards of twenty have already died, there were seven in one day.'"[1] Estabrook was the daughter of Perez and Lucinda Dickinson and the wife of Dr. Joseph Estabrook, who later became president of the University of Tennessee (UT).

In February 1850, a board of trustees led by East Tennessee University president William B. Reese was appointed to buy land and sell lots for a new cemetery. The other founding members were Marcus D. Bearden, James C. Moses, James M. Welcker, Joseph L. King, John H. Crozier and Perez Dickinson. The first land for the cemetery was purchased in December 1849. Making it official, an act passed by the Tennessee state legislature in February 1850 granted Old Gray's trustees authority to appropriate and dedicate real estate for a rural cemetery.[2] The first parcel of land purchased consisted of 8.0 acres about a mile northwest of the city's central business

Entrance gates. *Photo by Judy Loest.*

district for $500 from John Dameron. Dameron, originally from Virginia, had speculated correctly on Knoxville's coming growth and amassed a considerable amount of land north of the city. The plot to Old Gray was his first sale. Over the years, the cemetery made four more purchases, resulting in the current 13.47 acres.

The site of Old Gray was previously pastureland and had few trees, but over the years many trees have been planted, changing the landscape from an open pasture to a wooded garden and qualifying the site for certification as a Level I Arboretum. There are several trees over one hundred years old. Marble stones, made possible by the Akima Club and the Knoxville Garden Club, identify botanical and common names of over forty trees located at Old Gray. Cemetery board trustee and certified Master Arborist Jim Cortese inventoried and tagged all of Old Gray's trees.

There was a difference of opinion as to what would be an appropriate name for the new cemetery. Some favored Greenwood, some Woodlawn, others preferred Greendale and still others liked Fairview. At the suggestion of Reese's wife, Henrietta, the cemetery was named after English poet Thomas Gray (1716–1771), who wrote "Elegy Written in a Country Churchyard."[3] There was also some disgruntlement regarding the location. Only a mile from the city's downtown area, the location was considered ideal for a suburban cemetery, but a lot of people felt it was too far to visit.

Gray Cemetery was dedicated on June 1, 1852, with the sale of the first forty grave lots. The first burial had, however, occurred on July 15 of the previous summer, after a young local man named William Martin died of wounds from a cannon explosion during the city's Fourth of July celebration. Martin's grave, in the northwest section, remained unmarked until June 4, 2000, when a pink marble tombstone was installed to mark the sesquicentennial celebration of the founding of Old Gray.

In 1854, the Knoxville Board of Mayor and Aldermen and the different churches of the city were asked by the board of trustees of Gray Cemetery to procure grounds for the burial of their poor. This section is located near the south wall. During the Civil War, control of Knoxville shifted from Confederate to Union forces, and Old Gray, not yet surrounded by a fence, suffered damage from horses, wagons, men and cattle. Because of Knoxville's split allegiance, there are no political divisions within Old Gray—Union and Confederate soldiers, in equal numbers, are now peacefully at rest here.

The receiving vault was built in 1885. The same year, water from the city waterworks was brought to the cemetery. In 1890, the old stone wall along the Broad Street entrance was replaced with an iron fence. Also in 1890,

A.J. Albers had a large bronzed-iron fountain twenty feet high and weighing four tons erected in the center of the circle in memory of his wife. The Ella Albers Memorial Fountain, an iron and zinc fountain, was later removed due to rust and lack of money for upkeep and repairs. In 1949, board president William Rule Jr. solicited donations to establish a fund from which annual interest would pay for adequate maintenance. Prior to that, revenues came solely from burial fees, which grew smaller each year.[4]

The first sexton of the cemetery was Edmond Lavin (1797–1863), a native of Ireland. It was his responsibility to superintend the digging of all graves, for which he was paid two dollars each. After his death, his son John Lavin (1841–1903) became the second sexton. Both are buried at Old Gray. In 1897, a modern cemetery office, or "porter's lodge," was built from plans obtained from Knoxville architect Leon Beaver. It is a one-story building, rectangular in plan and constructed of Tennessee marble.

In 1900, New Gray Cemetery opened approximately three miles west, and Gray Cemetery became Old Gray. In 1902, the entrance posts were constructed following plans and specifications of Producers Marble Company of Knoxville for $650. The wrought-iron entrance gate was installed the following year. The west wall of five-foot-high concrete was built in 1907. The oldest fence in the cemetery is on the east side along Tyson Street (originally Holston Street). It was built in April 1890 by F.M. Arthur and Company for $0.94 per foot.

Burial records indicate that approximately 5,700 burials have been made in Old Gray Cemetery since it was founded. The monuments reflect the Victorian era when they were installed. Although there are some rectangular stone markers, the first impression one gets in the cemetery is of the elaborately shaped and carved monuments.

Strolling through Old Gray, one can imagine the changes brought by European immigration, war, epidemics and industrialization. And although Old Gray's circumference is small and one is never "far from the madding crowd's ignoble strife,"[5] time may still slow a bit on the border between two worlds.

2

OLD GRAY'S PLACE IN THE
GARDEN CEMETERY MOVEMENT

B y the 1840s, the garden cemetery movement (1833–75) and growing health concerns had influenced many U.S. urban planners to build larger, more elaborate cemeteries in their respective cities' outskirts and suburbs. The designs grew out of a romantic vision but were also spurred by necessity. The movement began with Cambridge's Mount Auburn Cemetery in 1831. That year, "the Massachusetts Horticultural Society purchased seventy-two acres of mature woodland situated in Watertown and Cambridge for the creation of a 'rural cemetery' and experimental garden. Their designers were inspired by English gardens and Père Lachaise in Paris. On September 24, 1831, a crowd of 2,000 gathered in the Dell, the natural amphitheater located in the heart of the Cemetery, for the dedication ceremony."[6] By 1848, the cemetery was welcoming sixty thousand visitors annually and newspapers were spreading its glories. In 1850, Parson Brownlow's *Whig* in Knoxville called Mount Auburn one of the most beautiful cemeteries in the world. During the weeks before Christmas in 1848, one of the recommended books for holiday gift-giving in major eastern U.S. cities, including Nashville, was *The Rural Cemeteries of America: Green-wood, Illustrated.*[7]

Old Gray's founders in 1850 didn't realize it at the time, but they created what would become Knoxville's first public park. By the 1860s, rural cemeteries could be found on the outskirts of cities and smaller towns across the country. The popularity of these cemeteries inspired the first public parks, and the public parks marked the demise of garden cemeteries. Frederick

Law Olmsted, famous landscape architect of Central Park, witnessing the throngs in rural cemeteries, concluded that cemeteries were at odds with "pleasure grounds," where people could enjoy nature without the gloom of death and also not interrupt mourners seeking quiet moments with lost loved ones. Over time, as public parks proliferated and burial became more sterile and efficient, cemeteries followed suit, designed primarily for the ease of mowers and automobiles.

Old Gray may be small at only 13 acres, but it has the distinction of being the second-oldest rural cemetery in the South, just behind Magnolia in Charleston, South Carolina, which was founded the same year, and one of only five in the South. The other three are Elmwood in Memphis (established in 1852, 80 acres) Metairie in New Orleans (1872, 150 acres) and Riverside in Macon, Georgia (1887, 54 acres).[8]

Today, as urban centers become more congested, the value of old garden cemeteries increases. Where public parks are often bustling with activities, the old cemeteries are often tranquil, offering a peaceful refuge in nature. They are good places to walk, read, write, study, meditate or just contemplate the long arc of a city's history. But now, with climate change, Old Gray offers something more. It adds to the city's network of green space infrastructure, providing cleaner air, trees to give shade and offset flooding and a haven for wildlife.

3

OLD GRAY AS A REFLECTION
OF KNOXVILLE'S MEDICAL HISTORY

The coronavirus pandemic reminds us that a pandemic and various epidemics were the reason Old Gray was founded in 1850. The plague of 1838, a fever of unknown cause, killed about 10 percent of Knoxville's population, many of whom are buried in the First Presbyterian Church Graveyard on State Street. Fetid millponds around First Creek were blamed, but that plague, coupled with annual epidemics of smallpox and typhoid, brought fears that graveyards might be the cause. Storm surges flooded the grounds, with gruesome results. An urgency arose in many American cities to establish cemeteries in surrounding countryside and thus independent from churches.

Because there were no vaccinations, many of the people buried in Old Gray died during these epidemics. In 1850, statewide deaths from a cholera epidemic ranged from 316 to about 500. In 1918, the Spanish flu pandemic is estimated to have killed almost 50 million people worldwide, two to four times the number killed in World War I. In Tennessee, 8,000 died, 1,300 in Nashville alone. According to the Centers for Disease Control (CDC), the 1918 pandemic lowered the national life expectancy by more than twelve years.

Other epidemics, such as diphtheria and scarlet fever, were also prevalent in Tennessee and often lasted as long as five years. Dysentery was common and could be fatal, and polio raged from 1915 to 1955. By 1943, the third-leading cause of death in Tennessee was tuberculosis. And child mortality was very high—in 1900, according to the CDC, one in five children "died

Knoxville General Hospital, 1917. *Photographs of Tennessee Cities Collection, Images of East Tennessee, University of Tennessee, Knoxville, Special Collections.*

during the first five years of life." Most deaths occurred at home without medical assistance. Premature deaths and funerals were so commonplace in the nineteenth century that Victorians established elaborate rituals around mourning as a way of maintaining a semblance of stability.

Knoxville's first hospital, City Hospital, opened in 1883 in the old Dr. Joseph Strong Home at what is now the corner of State Street and Cumberland Avenue. It was a makeshift operation with few beds.[9] Knoxville General Hospital opened in April 1902[10] just a block north of Old Gray and the National Cemetery. Founded amid complaints that it wasn't necessary and too expensive, the hospital proved indispensable in September 1904, when the New Market train wreck twenty-two miles northeast of Knoxville resulted in 64 fatalities and 141 injured.[11]

Like many growing cities in America, Knoxville was overwhelmed by the frequency of funerals and also tired of dreary Puritan cemeteries with their skulls and crossbones and gravestones carved with dire warnings like *momento mori* ("remember that you must die"). People lived with death and didn't need grim reminders. In 1831, a movement began to create beautiful rural garden cemeteries to help soften the frequent periods of mourning. Taking inspiration from Mount Auburn, Old Gray put a more comforting face on death.

Over time, as cleaner water and better hygiene arrived and as vaccinations and antibiotics became available, death was no longer a prime preoccupation. The first sewer systems in the state began in Memphis in 1879. The "sanitary movement" or the "public health campaign" emerged in the middle of the 1880s with prolific magazine advertisements of soap and other hygiene products. Handwashing and personal hygiene helped most cities in 1915 displace diarrhea as the leading cause of infant death in the United States.

Garden cemeteries like Old Gray came at a high cost but have lasting, inestimable value in the modern world. They serve to remind us of a universal pain—of loss, change and our shared inability to keep things from ending. But they but also remind us of how human ingenuity, invention and compassion can offer hope and alleviate much suffering and that beauty can be a balm.

4

RECEIVING VAULT

The receiving vault at Old Gray, designed by Knoxville architect Joseph F. Baumann, was built in 1885. The front was constructed of Tennessee marble, and the capacity of the ten-by-twelve-foot structure was ten to fifteen coffins. The main reason for receiving vaults was to temporarily store remains during winter, when the ground was too hard for graves to be dug by hand. It was also necessary to house and keep cool remains awaiting delayed funerals during summer months. Sometimes, even when a death occurred in Knoxville, the remains had to be held until remote family members could be reached for burial instructions or could arrive by train for the funeral, and this could take several days or weeks. On rare occasions, the funeral took place in the receiving vault.

A humorous story about the receiving vault appeared in a 1933 *Knoxville News-Sentinel* article. In it, longtime Old Gray gravedigger W.J. Lynch recounted the day a young man came into the cemetery and said he had heard there were corpses in the vault. He wanted to peep through the bars in the door, but Lynch told him he "didn't have the right to let him be disturbing the dead." Lynch watched the young man saunter toward the vault anyway and followed him. Lynch then climbed to the top, where the air-vent pipe rose from the earthen roof. When the man peeked in, Lynch spoke into the pipe, "Please, mister, go away and leave my bones alone." He watched as the young man lurched away and "then his knees just doubled up under him and down he went. I never saw a man as pale in my life; he looked like he was almost dead." Lynch felt bad and told

Receiving vault. *Photo by Judy Loest.*

the man, "Listen, mister, there's nothing in that place. That was just me a-talkin' into a pipe in the roof." "I knowed it," said the young man, "I just have a weak heart and can't stand any excitement."

Receiving vaults largely ceased to be built once powered digging equipment, such as the steam shovel and backhoe, came into use in the early 1900s. Today, Old Gray's receiving vault is used as storage for lawn equipment.

5

OLD GRAY'S ARBORETUM STATUS

In 2014, Old Gray, under the guidance of executive director Alix Dempster, was certified as a Level I Arboretum by the Tennessee Urban Forestry Council. Level I (out of four levels) requires a minimum of thirty labeled species of trees. Old Gray, with fifty-nine species, is close to achieving Level II status (sixty labeled species). In total, Old Gray has 411 trees, about 80 percent of which are, in descending order, magnolia, dogwood, crepe myrtle, maple, redbud, holly, walnut, ginkgo, oak and eastern red cedar. The trees are maintained and inventoried by Old Gray board member and professional arborist Jim Cortese.

Along with Old Gray's history and unique monuments, its diverse tree canopy is a vital component of this garden sanctuary. While the surrounding land is increasingly deforested and degraded, historic cemeteries provide small urban oases that have the potential to sustain biodiversity for many reasons. First, the trees are not disrupted by power lines, sidewalks, driveways or other urban features that impact their growth. Second, the trees are usually in soil that is free of pesticides. And third, the trees are often left alone, allowed to grow to their natural height and spread and then die naturally of old age. Untimely deaths among these trees are due to nature—lightning strikes and/or uprooting due to heavy rains or strong winds.

Old Gray, having previously been pastureland, was originally sparsely populated with trees. But due to its founding at the height of the garden cemetery movement (roughly 1830–70), it quickly transformed from an open pasture to a wooded garden. With the arrival of railroads in Knoxville and

Old Gray trees. *Photo by Judy Loest.*

increasing industrialization fueled by coal, air pollution made Old Gray a popular recreation venue for many residents in surrounding neighborhoods. It was a destination for social gatherings and picnics after church services on Sunday, for courting couples and for playing children.

Since most of the people buried in Old Gray were immigrants or children of immigrants, the trees reflect not only the East Tennessee landscape but also European landscaping preferences. Evergreen trees, especially conifers, universal symbols of immortality, have always been popular in cemeteries. On Old Gray's main drive, the beautiful old Norway spruce, native to the mountains of northern and central Europe, is an example of a tree that is green year-round. Other evergreens include hemlock, cedar, magnolia, holly and arborvitae (thuja). Another Old Gray tree that can be termed an evergreen is the large old water oak in the Tyson circle.

In particular is the large American sweet gum, which, in late summer and fall, attracts a large number of goldfinches. They can be seen flitting among the spiked balls, swinging and pecking in a flurry of activity. Each spiky ball contains two seeds, and although the sweet gum is a goldfinch magnet, other birds (purple finches, chickadees, Carolina wrens, towhees, titmice, doves and juncos) also consume the seeds, as do squirrels and chipmunks. At the same time as this activity, a flock of mourning doves can be seen feeding in the leaf debris piled along the curb below.

Beautiful old garden cemeteries like Old Gray are not just places for remembering the dead or breathing fresher air, they also improve one's mental health. The psychological benefits of trees are now well known. Trees screen or soften unattractive views, such as the harsh outline of masonry, metal, asphalt, steel and glass. They absorb sound waves, reducing noise pollution. Invisible benefits are even greater; studies have shown that trees slow heartbeats, lower blood pressure, improve concentration and induce more relaxed brain wave patterns.

As more urban tree canopy disappears, Old Gray, with social and governmental awareness and assistance, has the potential to contribute even more benefits to Knoxville's urban forest.

6

ELLA ALBERS MEMORIAL FOUNTAIN

In September 2018, Old Gray was proud to install an exact replica of the Albers Memorial Fountain, which had been missing for sixty-five years. The original fountain was donated to the cemetery in 1890 by Andrew Jackson "Jack" Albers, founder of one of Knoxville's oldest businesses, Albers Drug Company, in memory of his wife, Ella, who died at age thirty-seven. Through the decades, the fountain deteriorated due to rust and was eventually scrapped during a World War II metal drive.

The new seventeen-foot fountain was manufactured by Robinson Iron in Alexander City, Alabama. The Robinson pattern is likely a design made by J.W. Fiske and Company of New York City, one of the most prominent cast-iron companies in operation during the last half of the nineteenth century. Fiske's lavishly illustrated catalogs featuring fountain designs copied from the neoclassical sculptures of Italian Antonio Canova and Dane Bertel Thorvaldsen kept the company in the Victorian eye. The figures were molded in clay, then cast in plaster to provide the molds for the cast iron in a process similar to bronze-founding. Fiske also manufactured statues, urns, cast-iron furniture and, after the Civil War, monuments of dedication throughout the northern United States.

A similar Fiske fountain, the *Maids of the Mist*, made for the Chicago World's Fair and shipped to St. Joseph, Michigan, in 1892, was restored in 1974 and remains a popular photo subject for tourists. A three-tiered version with four maidens at the bottom, the "deluxe model" was restored by Robinson Iron in 2015 for a park in St. Albans, Vermont. Robinson Iron,

Ella Albers Memorial Fountain, twilight. *Photo by Judy Loest.*

Ella Albers Memorial Fountain, December 2019. *Photo by Judy Loest.*

which owns the original molds used to cast the St. Albans fountain, has restored two other of the original Fiske fountains.

Fiske made hundreds of these fountains, but only a handful have survived due to parts constructed of zinc and lead solder, which failed over time. Modern replications and restorations are made using materials and construction methods that endure the weather and plumbing-electrical systems that are more efficient.

A.J. Albers died in 1910 at age sixty-six and is buried alongside Ella. The new Albers Fountain waterworks were activated for the first time during the special dedication ceremony, and the fountain is operable for special events.

7

CEMETERY SYMBOLISM

CLUB, SOCIETY AND FRATERNITY SYMBOLS

From the mid-1800s to the mid-1900s, fraternal organizations held a place of prominence in most cities, and Old Gray reflects that tradition.

> *In the last two decades of the 19ᵗʰ century, Americans created almost 500 national fraternal beneficiary orders and thousands of local lodges....Because the Civil War provided the context for much of the mystery, excitement, and ritual surrounding fraternal organizations, they flourished and multiplied after its close. By the turn of the twentieth century, five million American men belonged to at least one fraternal organization....Approximately one-half of this enormous total were the three oldest and most purely fraternal—the Independent Order of Odd Fellows, the Freemasons, and the Knights of Pythias....They were not without controversy. Although fraternal organizations like the Masons sometimes crossed class, ethnic, and religious (but almost never racial) lines, they more often reinforced those divisions.* [12]

Freemasonry is the world's oldest and largest fraternal organization. Its members have included kings, presidents, prime ministers, politicians, Supreme Court justices, titans of industry, movie stars—and possibly your grandfather. Affiliates include Scottish Rite and Shriners International.

MISCELLANEOUS SYMBOLS

ANCHOR: Christ, who prevents people from becoming lost. Can also indicate that the deceased person was a sailor.

ANGEL: Spirituality. Angels guard the tomb, guide and pray for the soul and direct living visitors to think heavenward. The angel Michael bears a sword. The angel Gabriel blows a horn. A guardian angel is one without horn or sword.

ARCH: Ceremonial, victory, triumphant significance. Triumph over death, arch of sky and heaven, passage to heaven.

BED: Eternal sleep or rest.

BIRD: The soul.

BOOK: A stack of books indicates knowledge. An open book symbolizes the word of God revealed to the deceased.

CHERUB: Angelic, innocence. A cherub or baby angel is most often used on children's markers.

CELTIC CROSS: Circles symbolize eternity, sometimes linked with Celtic origins

COLUMN: Often used for war veterans. Multiple columns tied together represent members of a family. A broken column represents decay, usually indicating the loss of the family head.

DRAPERY: Sorrow and mourning.

FLOWER: Flower garlands indicate a pure life. Flower bouquet symbolizes grief. Lily is for purity. Morning glory indicates the beginning of a new life. Pansy is for remembrance. Rose symbolizes the Virgin Mary.

HANDS: Hands pointing up symbolizes the pathway to heaven. Hands clasped indicates marriage. Hands praying symbolizes asking God for eternal life. Hands blessing is used to indicate blessing of those left behind.

INSIGNIA: IOOF (Independent Order of the Odd Fellows), a fraternal organization. Most common symbol is a three-link chain with the initials F, L, T (friendship, love, truth). OES (Order of the Eastern Star), a women's organization. Symbol is a five-pointed star with a pentagon in the center containing an altar with an open Bible. SAR (Sons of the American Revolution). Symbols include an eagle sitting on top of a Maltese cross, often with the words *Libertas et patria*. VFW (Veterans of Foreign Wars) is symbolized by the Maltese cross. The Masonic Order, a fraternal organization, is symbolized by an inverted compass over a carpenter's square, often with a *G* in the middle. Also indicative of architects and surveyors. In ecclesiastic art, indicates divine measuring and dividing of

Cemetery symbolism (Nannie Meem tombstone). *Photo by Judy Loest.*

the world. WOW (Woodmen of the World), a fraternal society, now called WoodmenLife, known for grave markers shaped like logs or tree stumps.

LAMB: Most commonly found on nineteenth-century child grave markers, the lamb stands for innocence. Christians associate it with the Lamb of God (Jesus). A lamb with a banner signifies resurrection.

LAMP: Word of God; truth; good works; immortality of the spirit.

LETTER: AO (alpha and omega) refers to the beginning and the end and is often shown with the book of life. IHS indicates the first three letters in the Greek spelling of the name *Jesus*. XP, or *chi-rho*, are the first two Greek letters in the name *Christos* and refer to being buried under Christ. Today, the letters may be reversed (PX) to represent *pax* ("peace").

PLANTS: Ivy indicates friendship and fidelity. A thistle is used for Scottish descent and remembrance. A vine signifies a Christian church (wine signifies Jesus's blood). Wheat symbolizes divine harvest and death of an elderly person.

RING (BROKEN): The family has been severed.

ROCK: Steadfastness and stability.

ROPE: Eternity.

SCALES: Equality and justice. Archangel Michael is often portrayed holding a set of scales to weigh the souls of the departed. Use of scales can also display the occupation of the deceased.

SCROLL: Law or scriptures.

SCYTHE: Harvesting tool that represents death.

SEASHELL/SCALLOP SHELL: Earthly pilgrimage of human beings, or birth and resurrection.

SHEEP: Christians (Jesus is the shepherd).

SHIP: Occupation of the deceased, or the human journey through life.

SNAKE (WITH TAIL IN MOUTH): Everlasting life.

SUNDIAL: Nearness of death.

SWASTIKA: Swastikas sometimes appear on Celtic monuments. The swastika is one of the oldest and most widespread symbols. In early Celtic Christianity, it symbolized prosperity and good fortune. It derives from the Sanskrit *svastika* ("conducive to well-being)." It can be found on artifacts thousands of years old from several continents. While it was used by the Norse and other Germanic peoples from the beginnings of those societies, the swastika is far from just a Germanic symbol. It was one of the central symbols of Proto-Indo-European society, the society that gave rise to the Germanic, Celtic, Slavic, Greek and Roman societies in Europe, as well as Hindu societies in India, accounting for its use by both ancient and modern-day Hindus and Buddhists. Nor was it an exclusively Indo-European symbol. It can also be found in the indigenous art of the American Indians, the Sami of the far north of Scandinavia and other peoples around the world.

SWORD: Martyrdom, courage, warfare. Crossed swords indicate a military person of high rank.

THREE: As used in chains, points and leaves, indicates the Holy Trinity.

TORCH: A lit torch symbolizes life or eternal life. An extinguished torch means death, or living memory and eternal life. An elevated torch stands for resurrection. A lowered torch symbolizes death.

TREE: A tree growing from a tomb or an urn symbolizes rebirth. A fallen tree symbolizes death. A broken tree branch indicates mortality. A tree trunk symbolizes brevity (shortness) of life. A tree stump indicates a life interrupted.

URN: A broken urn symbolizes an elderly person. A draped and empty urn indicates that a soul has left the body. An urn with a flame means eternal remembrance.

WREATH: Ancient symbol for victory. In the Christian religion, a wreath symbolizes the victory of redemption.

There are many other features in Old Gray. Garden pieces, known as "cemetery furniture," became popular during the Victorian period. Many people would bring a picnic lunch to the cemetery and spend the day looking at the markers and relaxing in a park-like setting. Benches, small tables, planters, urns, fountains and bird baths—objects more commonly associated with gardens—were used to decorate grave sites and became features associated with the cemetery landscape. Cradle graves were often used for children, and toys were often left at the graves of children. Flowers serve as expressions of sympathy to the mourners and as tributes to the deceased. In the past, the importance of an individual was determined by counting the number of wagons and attendants used for flower delivery. Since the 1950s, artificial flowers have replaced fresh flowers and plants to a degree. The custom of leaving items on graves is still seen in many cultures. For example, a common item left on Jewish tombstones is a small stone or pebble.

8

OBELISKS

Obelisks have a long history as grave markers. An obelisk is a tapered, four-sided column that most commonly tapers off at the top into a pyramid shape, but it also may be draped or topped with objects such as urns, crosses or human figures. They were first used at Egyptian temples and later appeared in the mortuary complexes of pharaohs. In fact, the oldest, most authentic obelisk in the United States is Cleopatra's Needle, built between approximately 1500 and 1200 BC. It was brought from Alexandria, Egypt, and erected in Central Park in 1881. Probably the most notable obelisk in the nation is the 555-foot-tall Washington Monument in Washington, D.C., which was completed in two phases of construction, one private (1848–54) and one public (1876–84). As an aspect of Egyptian Revival architecture, obelisks became a popular form of cemetery/funerary art in the United States by the 1840s and continued to be used until about the 1920s. Following the expeditions that eventually led to the discovery in 1922 of the treasure of Tutankhamun's tomb by the archaeologist Howard Carter, the use of obelisks again flourished from 1920 to 1950.

Because Old Gray had many burials during those decades, it has several obelisks of different heights and designs. In fact, it's hard to find a cemetery from that period without one. Some of Old Gray's are plain, some are covered or draped, some are topped with an urn and some, like the Henry Richard Gibson monument, have a draped urn. The tallest obelisk in Old Gray, over fifty feet, is the monument of U.S. Navy lieutenant Charles McGhee Tyson, twenty-nine, who was killed in an airplane crash on a mission over the North

Sea in October 1918. A unique obelisk topped with a Roman figure is the monument of James Cowan, Knoxville merchant and the twenty-second and twenty-fifth mayor of Knoxville, and his wife, Lucinda Dickinson Cowan, daughter of Perez Sr. and Lucinda Dickinson. Other prominent obelisks are monuments of prominent Knoxvillians (Albers, Ault, Baumann, Briscoe, Jaques, McGhee, Staub and Temple). But all of the obelisks, even the most modest, represent an interesting story set in an interesting time in Knoxville's history.

WOODMEN OF THE WORLD TOMBSTONES

Old Gray has several examples of the unique tombstones known as "treestones." The use of treestones as grave markers arose in the 1800s, an outgrowth of the back-to-nature Victorian rustic rural cemetery movement. As a symbol of death and an image of nature, the treestone was a common choice from 1870 to 1920. For many cultures, the tree is a symbol of life. Conversely, a dead tree represents the opposite. Therefore, Victorian treestones were portrayed almost always as a dead tree trunk. Nevertheless, a stone trunk offered a warmer image than the ubiquitous vertical slabs found in most cemeteries. Often, as in the W.L. Murphy stone in Old Gray, the "tree" bark is "peeled back" so that a name, dates and/or epitaph could be engraved.

Many of Old Gray's treestones are associated with the Woodmen of the World Life Insurance Society (now officially WoodmenLife), a not-for-profit fraternal benefit society that operates a large privately held insurance company for its members. William Cullen Root founded Modern Woodmen of America (MWA) in Lyons, Iowa, in 1883 after hearing a sermon about "pioneer woodsmen clearing away the forest to provide for their families." In 1890, Root founded the life insurance society in Omaha, Nebraska. From 1890 until 1900, treestones were a benefit of membership. WOW members purchased a $100 rider to cover the cost of the monument. These distinctive headstones are found in cemeteries nationwide and are an enduring physical legacy of the organization.

Woodmen of the World, tree trunk monument. *Photo by Judy Loest.*

Treestones, as the name implies, are in the shape of a tree stump or stacked logs. The treestones of Woodmen will usually include its symbols—commonly trees, branches and/or leaves—and might be inscribed with the phrase *dum tacet clamet* ("though silent he speaks") or "here rests a Woodman of the World." Trees generally symbolize strength, longevity and/or immortality. A jagged and rough break marks the sudden, unexpected termination of a life cut short. Fern at the stone's base illustrates humility and sincerity. Sometimes, a bronze Woodmen plaque was attached at the base.

Most of these monuments were carved from Indiana limestone from Bedford, Indiana, the "limestone capital of the world." Master stone carvers came from Ireland, Scotland, France, Germany and Italy to work in the Indiana quarries. Naturally, some of the most elaborate treestones can be seen in Bedford's historic Green Hill Cemetery. Many of those early stone carvers are buried there near the Stone Cutters Monument, erected by the Bedford Stone Cutters Association in 1894. Many of the treestones in other states were carved by local carvers from WOW patterns.

As the Woodmen treestones became more popular, Sears, Roebuck and Company and Montgomery Ward began offering them for sale. The Woodmen benefit program eventually proved too costly and was abandoned in the late 1920s. Treestones are no longer available. In a 2000 *Knoxville News Sentinel* article by Don Ferguson, Ronnie Brimer, owner of Brimer Monument Company, said, "It would cost four fortunes to make one of those [treestones] today—probably $10,000. They were carved out of marble by hand. We use granite today, and it's all done with electric saws."

Woodmen social and civic activities were frequently reported in the *Knoxville News Sentinel* through the 1940s. Today, WoodmenLife's nearly 1,300 statewide chapters continue to conduct local community service projects, give scholarships to qualifying high school graduates and provide extra benefits to members who are nonmilitary first responders.

PART II

BIOGRAPHIES

DRURY PAINE ARMSTRONG FAMILY

The sleeping infant atop Amelia Franklin Armstrong's tombstone and the inscription below, as on so many Old Gray tombstones, are slowly being eroded. Amelia, born in 1857, died at less than two years of age. Not many people know of Amelia, but most know of her family, a prominent and influential one in Knoxville in the years before and after the Civil War. Following strands of Amelia's family tree leads to some interesting and notable local personalities.

Amelia was the first child of Robert Houston Armstrong and Louise Franklin and a granddaughter of Drury Paine Armstrong (1799–1856) and Amelia Houston (1805–1836). Beginning in 1832, Drury Armstrong established a gentleman's farm on six hundred acres along the Holston River. In a few years, he added three hundred acres on the south side of the river. Much or all of that property came to the Armstrongs as land grants for their service in the Revolutionary War. Drury named his house Crescent Bend (aka the Armstrong-Lockett House). In 1858, a year after Amelia's birth, Bleak House (aka Confederate Memorial Hall), named after the Charles Dickens novel, was built on Crescent Bend land donated by Drury. The house was a wedding gift for Robert and Louise Armstrong from Louise's father, Major Lawson D. Franklin. Major Franklin was a planter, slave trader and businessman and was the first millionaire in Tennessee. The Franklin home still stands in White Pine, Jefferson County, Tennessee.

One month to the day before Amelia died, Louise Armstrong gave birth to twin daughters, Ann Adelia and Elizabeth "Lizzie." Like Amelia, the twins were born on the Franklin Jefferson County estate. A fourth child, Robert Franklin Armstrong, was born five years later. In 1881, Lizzie married James

Paris McMillin (sometimes spelled McMillan) of Chattanooga, who died seven years later during a multibuilding fire in downtown Chattanooga. He was trying to save company books when burning walls collapsed. Lizzie died in 1895 at age thirty-five, cause unknown.

Amelia's sister Adelia became one of Knoxville's most well-known artists. She studied impressionism in Paris, taught painting for several years in Knoxville and exhibited nationally. Adelia married John Lutz in 1886, and they built historic Westwood on Kingston Pike, not far from Bleak House and Crescent Bend.

In 1902, Robert "Bob" Franklin Armstrong married Annie Wetzell, whose family had moved from Grand Rapids, Michigan, to Knoxville in 1885. Her father, Henry B. Wetzell, served as a broker for a British mineral and timber company. Anne often accompanied her father into the mountainous regions of Tennessee and developed a deep love of the region. Henry, according to a tribute in the March 1894 issue of the *Wood Worker* journal, to which he contributed many articles, was held in high regard.

> *In speaking of the late Henry B. Wetzell of Knoxville, Tennessee, a friend refers to his popularity among the mountaineers of Kentucky, Tennessee and North Carolina. Of the latter it is said if they knew that if he was coming amongst them, they would gather in the evening for miles around to greet him and listen to him. He was almost the only man in the world whom the moonshiners of NC would allow into their retreats, because they respected his personal bravery and knew that however much he might object to their lawlessness, he would never betray their hospitality; they trusted him....Modest, broad-minded, intelligent, patient and affectionate, and brave until the very end...[he was] a worthy representative of the best element[s] of character.*

Henry was almost crushed to death in an 1889 railway accident near Flat Creek in Grainger County, Tennessee, and suffered from his injuries until his death five years later at age fifty-one.[13] The family's wealth soon declined, but Anne was able to attend Mount Holyoke College. She had returned to Knoxville by 1892, when she married Leonard Waldron, with whom she had one child, Roger. They divorced in 1894. After her divorce from Waldron, Anne supported her infant son and parents by teaching school in Knoxville.

Bob Armstrong would also go on to have a short-lived marriage, to his cousin Celia Houston. Marrying cousins was still common at the time.

Drury and Amelia were also cousins. After his divorce, Bob spent five years in the Dakotas as an inspector for the commissioner of the Bureau of Indian Affairs. It is said that the store windows along Gay Street were filled with the many Indian artifacts Bob brought back on his return.

Based on her first impressions of Bob during a Sunday service in the First Presbyterian Church of Knoxville, which she described in an unfinished memoir, the fifteen-year-old Anne seemed to have intuited their coming union. She wrote that her heart "gave a leap…upon seeing this dare-devil of dare-devils, the Armstrongs' erratic and picturesque son," who "was above everything else very much a man.…[H]ow startled I would have been had some voice whispered that in future years the life of this man would be intricately intertwined with my own."[14]

Anne and Bob married on June 14, 1905, in Washington, D.C., and she soon became a pioneering businesswoman. She attended the University of Chicago, held management positions with the National City Company on Wall Street and Eastman Kodak in Rochester and published several articles about the emergence of women in the business world. She was the first woman to lecture at the Harvard and Dartmouth Schools of Business. Bob continued to be a traveling salesman.

In the late 1920s, after moving about for several years, Anne and Bob settled at Knobside, a large log home overlooking the Holston River in the Big Creek community near Bristol, Tennessee, in Sullivan County. There they enjoyed the slow pace and scenic beauty of the area. Anne concentrated on her writing, making Knobside the setting for her novel *This Day in Time*. Bob ceased traveling and became a bird enthusiast.

They lived there until Bob's death of a heart attack in 1931. His death certificate gave his profession as "naturalist," and his obituary stated that he had come "to Big Creek for peace and contentment after a life spent at various times on a plantation, among Indians, and as a traveling salesman."[15]

In the spring of 1937, in Asheville, Anne met and began a correspondence with novelist Thomas Wolfe. Wolfe, a native of that city, had just returned home after a long exile and, due to his fame, found the visit a "three-ring circus." He found respite in friends' remote cabins. Anne offered him her younger sister's

Anne W. Armstrong's 1924 passport photo. *WikiMedia, Creative Commons Attribution-Share Alike 3.0 Unported.*

cabin next to Knobside. In September of that year, he accepted the offer and spent a week there, at the end of which Anne drove him to Marion, Virginia, to spend a few days with novelist Sherwood Anderson.

Anne remained at Knobside until the mid-1940s, when the Tennessee Valley Authority (TVA) flooded the river to construct a dam, a lake and a reservoir. Not only Knobside but also the fabled Big Creek community now lie at the bottom of South Holston Lake. As reported in the article "Secrets of Big Creek Revealed" in the *Bristol Herald Courier* of April 2019, Anne's sister's house, very similar to Knobside, was constructed in 1933 and, in 1942, was removed and reassembled in Bristol.

After moving about to several places in the Southeast, Anne finally settled in Abingdon, Virginia, and lived at the Barter Inn until her death in 1958. The inn, established in 1935 to house actors, was originally the Stonewall Jackson Female Institute, which closed in 1930. Actors received no pay but were well fed and given rent-free rooms in the college dormitories. The inn also provided a number of reservations for the public.

Anne Armstrong has never garnered the recognition she deserves and is less well known in her hometown than is her sister-in-law Adelia, but scholars of southern and Appalachian literature have been discovering her. In 2019, she was inducted into the East Tennessee Writers Hall of Fame. A 350-page fragment of her unfinished autobiography, *Of Time and Knoxville*, which focuses on her life in Knoxville between 1885 and 1902, is in the Archives of Appalachia at East Tennessee State University.

Robert Houston Armstrong and Louise Armstrong are also buried in Old Gray, as are Henry and Lorinda "Linnie" Wetzell. Adelia and John Lutz are buried in Berry Highland Cemetery on Sutherland Avenue. Lizzie and James McMillin are buried in Forest Hills Cemetery in Chattanooga. Anne and Bob are buried in Rooty Branch Baptist Church Cemetery in Bristol, Tennessee. This cemetery was used as the final resting place for the majority of the relocation burials from the South Holston Lake TVA Project for this entire region. TVA's Cemetery Relocation Program archive shows that R.F. Armstrong was originally buried in the Armstrong Cemetery, likely a family plot on Knobside property. Anne's date of death was never carved on her tombstone, but the title of her novel, *This Day in Time*, is.

ELEANOR DEANE SWAN AUDIGIER

Eleanor "Ella" Deane Swan Audigier (1864–1931) was born in Knoxville on May 17, 1864. Her father, Matthew Dodson Swan, served as Knoxville sheriff (1874–76). Ella exhibited a love of art at an early age and pursued it all her life. At some uncertain date in her youth, she may have studied at the Art Students League in New York City with sculptors Daniel Chester French and Augustus St. Gaudens. She published articles and delivered lectures on art and her travels to fellow members of the Ossoli Circle, the oldest General Federation Women's Club in the South. She was a founding member of Knoxville's Nicholson Art League and served as its leader from 1906 to 1923. Notable members of the league were artists Lloyd Branson, Catherine Wiley, Adelia Armstrong Lutz and Charles Krutch, photographer Joseph Knaffl and architect George Franklin Barber. Eleanor served as secretary for the Fine Arts Section of the Appalachian Exposition of 1910. She is listed among "Who's Who in Art" in the 1917 and 1918 editions of the *American Art Directory*.

In 1888, Eleanor married Louis Bailey Audigier, a newspaper editor from Little Rock, Arkansas, who was part owner of the S.B. Newman Printing Company in Knoxville. They bought Crescent Bluff, the previous home of Virginia Rosalie and Joseph Carson Coxe, which stood on Kingston Pike between historic homes Crescent Bend and Bleak House. Coxe, then a widower, continued to live at Crescent Bluff and traveled with the Audigiers. Eleanor settled into her role as arts patron, and Louis became a poultry expert, serving as president of the Tennessee branch of the American Poultry Association and editing and printing a newspaper, the *Industrious Hen*, the leading poultry journal of the South. In 1911, the house, in a far west area without fire protection, burned to the ground, destroying a large library and art collection.[16]

The Audigiers shared a great interest in Italy, its culture and art, and soon after the fire, they and Coxe left Knoxville to travel in Europe, Asia and Africa. They spent the winter of 1911 and 1912 in Egypt, the greater part of the time in Cairo and Luxor studying ruins, visiting museums and excavations and making sketches. After their grand tour, they settled in Italy and lived there for a quarter of a century, including for a time in Florence but mostly in Rome, where they had a suite at the Grand Continental Hotel. There, Eleanor assembled her collection of antique objets d'art and sent personal letters and long reports to the Nicholson Art League, which called her "our foreign correspondent." During that time, Louis was a Rome photographic correspondent for the *New York Times*.

Before their departure for Europe, Eleanor was instrumental in devising a curriculum for the Nicholson Art League and creating its motto: "It has been the office of art to educate the perception of Beauty." (The quote comes from Ralph Waldo Emerson in his 1841 collection of essays.) The League flourished for almost twenty-five years but gradually lost relevance and funding due to the deaths or relocations of major early founders and radical art movements such as cubism, futurism and surrealism that were at odds with the League's devotion to French Impressionism and the Italian Renaissance. Around 1930, the club changed its name to the Knoxville Art League, purchased Melrose Place and began a fund drive to turn the building into the Melrose Art Center.[17] But the Great Depression hit. In 1932, the old home was converted into duplex apartments.[18] Around 1961, the house was demolished to make way for a new men's dormitory on the UT campus.[19]

Eleanor Audigier monument, Madonna sculpted in Italy. *Photo by Judy Loest.*

Eleanor died in Rome on August 26, 1931. Her health had been in decline for several years, conditions attributed to her three years (1914–17) as a volunteer in the World War I women's war relief efforts in Rome. At the outset of the war, she volunteered for such duties as making bandages and assisting in a hospital. In 1917, the Austrian military broke through Italy's northeastern Alpine border, forcing five hundred thousand refugees to flee south, a mass exodus that created chaotic conditions in Italy. The U.S. ambassador to Italy, Thomas Nelson Page, organized a system of charity, and his wife, Florence Page, marshaled American women living in Rome. Working alongside the American Red Cross, volunteers assisted Italian soldiers, their families and refugees.[20] In 1916, Eleanor wrote to Knoxville friends describing her wartime experiences.[21]

Eleanor's remains, accompanied by Louis, arrived via ocean liner in New York on September 14 and came by train to Knoxville. In 1932, Louis donated a sculpture of Leonardo da Vinci's *The Last Supper* to Church Street Methodist Church, the church of Ella and her mother. The five-by-three-foot bas-relief was carved from Carrara marble by Pietro Bibolotti of Pietrasanta, Italy.

In 1933, Louis married Carol "Carro" Mae Hase of Arkansas, and in 1934, he donated Eleanor's extensive art collection to the University of Tennessee. In 1936, Louis bought the old Cochran home at 2651 East Magnolia, and the couple returned to Knoxville.[22] The old home still stands, but time and "progress" have altered its old elegance. The Audigier collection, which comprises over five thousand art objects, photographs and postcards, is housed in the McClung Museum on the University of Tennessee–Knoxville campus. The collection includes a pictorial record in postcards, luggage and hotel labels of their tour of the Nile Valley in 1912–13. Details of the Audigiers' grand tour can be read at the McClung Museum of Natural History and Culture at UT.

The beautiful Madonna over Eleanor's grave is a favorite of Old Gray visitors. The September 4, 1931 issue of the *Knoxville News Sentinel* noted, "Two years ago, Mrs. Audigier picked a monument of Italian marble and sent it to Knoxville for her burial lot." It is possible the monument also came from the Bibolotti studio, since brothers Antonio and Pietro Bibolotti also carved funerary sculpture for the North American market. The inscription reads, "Peace I leave with you, my peace I give unto you," the opening lines of John 14:27. The monument is shared by Eleanor's parents, Matthew Swan and Samantha Baker Swan, and Matthew's first wife, Cecilia Garrison Swan. Louis Audigier died in 1943 and is buried with Carro near the family home in Little Rock, Arkansas.

FERNANDO CORTES BEAMAN AND MARY JANE SHERROD BEAMAN

Fernando Cortes Beaman (1836–1911) was born in Burke, Franklin County, New York, the son of Timothy Olcott Beaman and Rebecca Allen, natives of Vermont. Timothy was a sixth-generation American whose ancestors emigrated from Shropshire, Staffordshire, England, and settled in Massachusetts in 1635. When the Civil War began, Fernando was a student at Middlebury College in Middlebury, Vermont, but he left in October 1861, three months before graduating, to enlist in the Ninety-Eighth New York Volunteer Infantry. He was wounded on May 16, 1864, at Drewry's Bluff, Virginia, and mustered out as a captain in the fall of 1865 in Richmond. He settled in East Tennessee and, in 1866, began teaching at the Rocky Springs Academy in Sevier County.[23]

Mary Jane Sherrod was the daughter of Charlotte Bales (1812–1860) and Jonathan Sherrod (1813–1953). The Sherrods were descendants of Arnholtz Sherertz (or Scherertz) of Rhineland, Prussia (now West Germany), who, along with his wife and five sons, immigrated to America in 1754. They settled in York County, Pennsylvania, and changed their surname, first to Sherrold, then to Sherrod. Mary Jane's grandfather Henry Sherrod moved to Sullivan County, Tennessee, in 1798. Her father, Jonathan Sherrod, married Charlotte Bales of Strawberry Plains, where they established a farm. Tragically, Jonathan died in 1853 at age thirty-nine. Mary was three, and her mother was four months pregnant with the sixth child, daughter Laura. Her mother died seven years later, leaving Mary, age ten, her seven-year-old sister Laura and her four older brothers (twenty, seventeen, fifteen and thirteen) to manage the farm.

Fernando and Mary, ages thirty-two and eighteen, respectively, were married on February 3, 1868, and established a farm in Strawberry Plains. According to frequent notices in the *Knoxville Weekly Chronicle*, Fernando continued to teach at other small schools in the area over the next decade, such as Cedar Grove High School in New Market; Lyons' Creek Academy in Strawberry Springs in 1871 ("assisted by his wife"); Thorn Grove Institute, where he boarded students in his home; Whortleberry Springs School in Strawberry Plains in 1873 (again, "assisted by his wife"); and, in 1874, Huckleberry Springs Normal School, ten miles east of Knoxville. A normal school was an institution created to train high school graduates to be teachers by educating them in the norms of pedagogy and curriculum. Fernando taught ten months a year for $600 a year.

In 1875, along with his brother Orin Beaman and Charles Burke of New York, Fernando bought 1,100 acres in east Knoxville from Alexander McMillan, property that had been a Revolutionary War land grant. He and his family moved into a log house on the property and started a dairy farm. In 1876, he filled the chair of ancient languages at Grant Memorial University in Athens, Tennessee, now East Tennessee Wesleyan, leaving his wife in charge of the dairy farm. He taught in Athens for four years, and Mary apparently did quite well managing the dairy in his absence. The 1883 Knoxville City Directory shows the Beamans living at "Milk Depot," 38 Vine Street. A "milk depot" was a facility for storing milk for distribution to individual consumers and retailers.

In 1885, after buying out his partners, Fernando conceived the idea of a pleasure park on forty-five acres of his pastureland. In 1886, he began forming a lake, which he named Lake Ottosee, a contraction for "the lake you ought to see." Two of the first structures he built were a boathouse and a dancing pavilion. He soon added mineral springs, and the area was known for a number of years as Beaman's Park. In 1889, he arranged with the city of Knoxville to extend a trolley line, the first to be powered electrically and not by mules, to the park, which he renamed Chilhowee.

Chilhowee became a popular destination and was thronged by thousands on July 4 celebrations. On June 30, 1892, the Morristown, Tennessee *Herald and Tribune*, still using the name Lake Ottosee Park, announced the program for the day's events. The East Tennessee, Virginia and Georgia Railway was offering advance excursion tickets to Knoxville from all points on the line. In addition to biking, boating and swimming races, there would be "a balloon ascension by a professional lady aeronaut, Mlle. Leona, who will ascend to the height of 5,000 feet and leap, head first, with a parachute to the ground…plus a hundred other entertainments," ending with fireworks displays in the evening. Leona Dare, a trapeze-aerial acrobat known for hanging by her teeth from high wires and balloons, had performed at the Crystal Palace in London and the Folies Bergère in Paris. Even nearing the end of her career (she retired around 1894–95) and no longer hanging by her teeth, she was quite the headliner for Knoxville's little pleasure ground.

In the early 1900s, Chilhowee hosted many fairs and exhibitions. At the 1903 Labor Day Fair, the Baums, a bicycling aerialist duo, performed there, suspended two hundred feet on a wire. In 1913, the National Conservation Exhibition was held there. The September 16, 1919 *Maryville Times* announcing the October 1919 East Tennessee Division Fair declared the site "one of the best equipped and most attractive fair grounds in the entire South." In 1916, Chilhowee hosted the first East Tennessee Division Fair, which was renamed the Tennessee Valley Agricultural and Industrial Fair in 1932 and is an annual event today. And there were countless recreational events, including dances, concerts, vaudeville plays, picnics, fireworks, baseball games and horse shows.

Chilhowee was also the site of terrible accidents. In July 1896, a conveyance on the newly erected "Shoot the Chute" carrying thirteen children on a Sunday school picnic crashed into a rowboat carrying two young couples who were on a church picnic outing. No children were hurt, but the rowboat was splintered, and the passengers were thrown violently into the lake. Three of the young people died and were buried in Gray Cemetery.[24] In 1904, a young woman on a swing was fatally struck by a stray bullet from the shooting gallery. In 1918, Chilhowee played a part in World War I when the

Bandstand at Chilhowee Park.
Photograph by James E. Thompson,
Calvin M. McClung Historical
Collection, Knox County Public Library.

grounds were used as a military housing and training camp for new recruits. By early October, nearly two hundred soldiers had contracted the flu.

Over the course of forty years, the Beamans educated, supplied milk to and entertained East Tennesseans. Mary Beaman was a partner in all of these enterprises in addition to bearing nine children in twenty-two years, the last in 1891, when she was forty-one. She died in 1901 of tuberculosis at age fifty-one. Fernando Beaman lived to see the first Appalachian Exposition held at Chilhowee Park in 1910. He died at the home of his daughter on Rutledge Pike on August 19, 1911, at age seventy-four. The bandstand at Chilhowee, constructed of Tennessee marble for the exposition, is the only building still standing from that time.

MARY BELLE BEARDEN BARRY

Belle Bearden Barry (1856–1955) was the daughter of Benjamin Franklin Bearden and Rebecca Jane Smith. She married Isaac Eblen Barry Jr. (1852–1928), on September 8, 1875. They had one child, Bella Rosa, who married Dr. Henry Joseph Smith of Memphis in 1914. Isaac was the owner of I.E. Barry & Company Fruits and Confections at 117 Gay Street, a business he inherited from his father, Isaac Sr. The May 3, 1887 *Daily Sentinel* featured a lengthy article about "the finest soda fount in the South" currently being installed at I.E. Barry & Co., a marvel of construction featuring fifteen kinds of Belgian, French, Mexican and Tennessee marble, African onyx and containing thirty-five kinds of syrups and twenty-three mineral waters.

Belle Bearden Barry

Mary Belle Bearden Barry.
Findagrave.com.

The Barrys built an imposing red frame house at 823 West Main Avenue, near the L&N underpass on property that was Isaac's homestead.[25]

Belle was a poet and the author of *Whispers* (1905), a collection of poems about love and friendship, nature and childhood. She also published poems and essays in magazines, including the *Chilhowee Echo: A Woman's Journal.* Her poems were mostly simple, sentimental rhymed couplets, often with emphasis on religious virtues. In the early 1900s, her poems appeared frequently in the *Knoxville Journal and Tribune* and in a *Knoxville News Sentinel* column, Verse or Worse. She was also one of 36 Tennessee poets and 2,281 poets overall represented in *The North American Book of Verse* (1939). Zollie Howard, the *Knoxville News Sentinel* columnist, reckoned that the five-volume set would have "at least 2281 readers."[26]

In October and November 1909, Belle and Isaac traveled west by train, and many of her impressions from that trip resulted in her sixteen-page poem *Western Glimpses* (1910). The book is prefaced by a note from Belle to Adolphus Busch, thanking him for his vast gardens in Pasadena, which impressed her greatly. The Pasadena Busch Gardens, which opened in 1906, was one of America's earliest theme parks. Built by flamboyant brewer Busch on thirty-eight acres of land near his winter home, Ivy Wall Villa on Orange Grove Avenue, the gardens were a popular tourist attraction for thirty years. After Adolphus died, his wife, Lily Anheuser Busch, tried to give the gardens to the city, but the city refused. The lands were absorbed into an upper-class neighborhood. Remnants of the old gardens can be seen on certain private lots.

Belle also wrote music for the hymn "Philathea-Philathea" (1907), which was published in the *Adult Bible Class Hymnal.*[27] The Adult Bible Class was a central part of the Baraca and Philathea Union, founded in 1890 in association with the First Baptist Church of Syracuse, New York. The group began as a men's Bible class called Baraca (from the Old Testament word for blessing), and the women's group, Philathea ("lovers of God" in Greek), was formed in 1893. The Philathea became a women's movement in which classes were recruiting stations for indifferent and unchurched young women and girls of the community.[28] The extent of Belle's involvement with Philathea is unknown, but the notice of her death in the *Knoxville News Sentinel* stated that "she taught the Barry Bible Class for some 50 years at First Baptist Church here."

Belle died at the home of her daughter Mrs. Bella Rosa Barry Smith in Memphis, where she had lived the previous eight years. She was ninety-eight years old. Also buried in the Barry plot are Isaac, his parents, several of his aunts and uncles and Joseph and Bella Rosa Smith.

ORA BREWSTER BLANTON

Ora Brewster (1858–1890) was born in Grainger County, Tennessee, to Elizabeth "Eliza" Mayes and John Brewster. John was killed in a steamboat disaster on the Mississippi River sometime during or soon after the Civil War. In 1867, Eliza and her three daughters—Ora (eight), Mary "Mollie" (six) and Valeria "Vallie" (two)—moved from Grainger County, Tennessee, to Sweetwater, Tennessee, where Eliza's younger brother Henry Mayes and sister Mrs. E.A. Taylor and families lived.[29]

The move appears to have been a good one for Ora. Henry Mayes was a founder and beloved member of the Sweetwater community. Because the stage road ran directly by the Mayes home, it was a popular stopping and feeding place. The Mayeses were also a musical family, so it was natural that Ora, apparently a musical prodigy, pursued her love of piano. She was said to have had the gift of absolute pitch, able to tell instantly what note was struck on any instrument and as many as eight notes struck simultaneously if on a piano that was in good tune and one that she was accustomed to. She was an accomplished sight reader and could reproduce any short piece of music she heard if she could go to a piano at once.[30]

As the oldest child, Ora may have been forced to work to help support the family. But with her musical talent, she may have had ambition beyond the domestic sphere at a time when women were flocking to teaching, a profession that had theretofore been dominated by men. In any case, she taught music for ten years before marrying. She was the head of the music department at Thomasville Female College in Thomasville, North Carolina, from 1875 to 1880 and taught music at the Shelby Female Academy in Shelby, North Carolina, from 1881 to 1885. The June 9, 1881 *Carolina Watchman*, reporting on the Thomasville College concert the previous evening, stated, "The piano solos were entertaining and brilliant, reflecting much credit and praise upon Miss Ora Brewster, both as a musician of merit and as possessing that happy quality of imparting knowledge to others."

According to Knoxville newspaper "Personal" columns, Ora and her Sweetwater cousin, Jennie Mayes, frequently took the train to Knoxville. Catching the early morning East Tennessee, Virginia and Georgia train, they would have arrived in Knoxville in a little under an hour and departed on the morning train to Sweetwater the next day. They usually stayed overnight at Hattie House or the Lamar House Hotel. In June 1882, the *Knox Daily Chronicle* shared a clip from the *Monroe Democrat* stating that "Miss Ora Brewster has gone up to Knoxville for two weeks of post-graduate musical instruction under Prof. Knabe." Gustav Knabe, a German immigrant and graduate of the Leipzig Conservatory, was known in Knoxville as "a master and an authority in all matters relating to music." In 1869, he organized the University of Tennessee's cadet all-cornet marching band and served as its director for some twenty years. The band became part of the ROTC program at UT and in 1950 was named "The Pride of the Southland."[31]

Ora once participated in a "Blind Tom" Wiggins performance. Thomas Wiggins (1849–1908) was born into slavery in Georgia and by age three was recognized as a musical prodigy and likely autistic savant. He was sold as an infant to a Columbus, Georgia lawyer and in the family home was exposed to musical instruments and instruction. He became popular touring the South before and after the Civil War. His performances invariably contained a challenge, in which an audience member was brought onstage to play the most difficult piece of music he or she could. Blind Tom would stand by, wringing his hands and making improbable one-footed leaps in the air, anticipating the challenge and naming each note as it was played. He then retook the piano and played the piece back exactly as he had heard it, flaws and all. He could also play different pieces of music with each hand while singing a third, all in different keys.[32]

At some point in her North Carolina tenures, Ora met Charles "Charlie" Coleman Blanton (1857–1944) in Shelby, North Carolina. Charles was born in Shelby and, like so many young men after the Civil War, had followed another Blanton relative to Texas to seek his fortune. From all accounts, he seems to have quickly become successful there in hardware and dry goods, cattle, pharmaceuticals and banking. Ora and Charles married in July 1885 in Sweetwater and soon afterward moved to Meridian, Texas, where Charles took up banking, his father's profession.

Ora Brewster Blanton.
Photo by Judy Loest.

On January 28, 1890, the *Dallas Morning News* reported that Ora had died in Atlanta, Georgia, the previous morning. "The news of her death was a shock to her numerous friends here. A genuine sorrow is expressed at her death, and her memory will be cherished by all who value excellence in character." The death certificate listed the cause of death as consumption, the term for tuberculosis. According to her Knoxville obituary, Ora had suffered for years and had gone to Atlanta for treatment.[33]

Tuberculosis had grieved this family before. Eliza's brother in Sweetwater, Henry Mayes, lost his first wife to TB in 1857 and his daughter Mary in 1859. Mrs. Mayes and seventeen-year-old Mary were the primary caregivers to M.C. Parker, the local doctor who was a boarder in the Mayes home when he contracted the disease. Dr. Parker also died.

Ora was only thirty-one. She and Charles had been married for just four and a half years. There were no children. On June 30, 1894, TB struck again. This time, it was Ora's sister Vallie, twenty-eight, who died, leaving one child, a ten-year-old son. Charles returned to Shelby around 1895 to join his brother George in their father's banking firm. He never remarried, lived with George and his mother-in-law in the old family home and became the fourth bank president in the Blanton family.

The historic Blanton family home, now a reception venue called the Banker's House, was home to three generations of Blantons. As banking partners, Charles and his brother George seem a composite model for the character George Bailey (Jimmy Stewart) in the movie *It's a Wonderful Life*. The book *The Heritage of Cleveland County* quotes from a tribute by Dr. Zeno Wall at First Baptist Church, where Charles was a lifelong member:

> *When the banks were closed all of the country in 1933,* [Mr. Charlie's] *banks had to close but not for long. He and his brother George moved swiftly and sacrificially. They mortgaged over one half million dollars of their property in order that their banks might reopen, and he gave $100,000 in order that the depositors might sustain no losses. He and his brother George saved our banks and places of business, and restored confidence in the people. By every measure, he was an outstanding man. We shall greatly miss him and may never see his likes again.*

Charles remained active in the Shelby community for over forty years. He died in Marion, North Carolina, in 1944, at the age of eighty-six and is buried in Sunset Cemetery in Shelby with other Blanton family members. Mary "Mollie" Brewster died in 1872 at age ten and is buried in West View Cemetery in Sweetwater. Valeria "Vallie" died in 1894, also of consumption, age twenty-eight, and is buried in Old Gray along with her husband, Knoxville dentist A.R. Melendy, and their son, Melville. Ora's mother, Eliza, died in North Carolina on February 1, 1917, and is also buried in Old Gray.

DANIEL BRISCOE

Daniel Briscoe (1843–1918) was born in Greene County, Tennessee, on June 7, 1843, to Phillip Jackson and Martha Briscoe, natives of Mississippi and East Tennessee, respectively. He attended the public schools in Canton, Mississippi, and finished his education at the University of Mississippi in Oxford in 1861. In 1862, at the outbreak of the Civil War, he enlisted as a volunteer in the Eighteenth Mississippi infantry and was assigned to the quartermaster department located in Knoxville, Greeneville and Bristol, Tennessee. In 1864, at age twenty-one, he married Catherine C. Earnest and, at the close of the war, engaged in the retail mercantile business in Morristown, Tennessee, with his father-in-law, Joseph H. Earnest. They continued successfully for sixteen years. Joseph Earnest died in 1878. In 1882, Daniel came to Knoxville and, with his younger brother Phillip Jackson Briscoe, entered the jobbing business. Together, they founded Daniel Briscoe, Bro. & Company, wholesale merchants.

By 1896, Knoxville was the third-largest wholesaling center in the South, and Gay Street from Union to Jackson was filled with warehouses. Briscoe & Company, which wholesaled dry goods, notions, furnishings and ready-to-wear, was one of the state's leading firms. But success did not come without major losses. The first occurred on June 27, 1890, when the just-completed building that housed the Briscoe firm collapsed, damaging $200,000 worth of goods. The cause of the collapse was discovered a few days later, when a large cave was found beneath the center of the building. Briscoe sold his salvaged goods at less than half price, relocated to his old building on Gay Street and was in New York the following day replenishing his stock. The worst event was in April 1897, when Knoxville's "million-dollar" fire gutted the 300 block of Gay Street, and Briscoe lost a five-story building and over $300,000 of stock.

Daniel and Catherine had eleven children. Catherine died in 1883, and in 1889, Briscoe married Lucy Gillespie White (1862–1943). They had two children. Briscoe was a director of the East Tennessee National Bank and a member of the Masonic fraternity and the Presbyterian Church. In 1900, he bought the stately 1879 mansion built by James D. Cowan, another important Knoxville merchant and a leader in the city's post–Civil War recovery. The estate occupied the entire block on the corner of White and Cumberland. The main residence was a three-story brick house surrounded by a carriage house, greenhouses and the gardener's cottage.*

Briscoe retired in 1909. In September of that year, he and Lucy and their two children made a grand tour of the West. The Briscoe wholesale company reorganized and moved to a new Jackson Avenue location. The firm was finally liquidated in 1932. Briscoe died at home on February 6, 1918. His six surviving sons served as pallbearers at his funeral. His obituary in the February 17, 1918 *Knoxville Sentinel* lauded him as the city's merchant prince who "established a reputation for successful merchandising that has rarely been equaled anywhere."

Five of Daniel's children with Catherine are also buried in Old Gray. Lucy and the last two Briscoe children are buried in Westview Cemetery in Atlanta, Georgia.

*Nothing remains of the old Cowan-Briscoe mansion except the gardener's cottage, which has an interesting story. The Italianate-style cottage probably served as home to the Cowan's gardener, Michael Hoey, brought from England to oversee the gardens and greenhouses. The entire property was purchased by the University of Tennessee in 1920, and in 1925, the mansion became the university's first dormitory for women, Sophronia Strong Hall. The residence was demolished in 1954 and replaced by new Strong and Clement Halls. The modest gardener's cottage, protected over decades of change, is now the second-oldest building on campus. It was restored in 2017 and is now used as a student-oriented space for classes, meetings and occasional exhibitions.

EDITH CAULKINS

One of Old Gray's cradle graves belongs to Edith Caulkins (1887–1918), whose story takes us to Jamaica and revisits the 1918 Spanish flu epidemic. Edith's parents were Dr. Douglas Caulkins (1858–1936) and Lucy Jane Tydeman Caulkins (1861–1949). Lucy was born in Jamaica, where her English parents, William Watson Tydeman (1824–1898), a doctor of homeopathic medicine, and Letitia Jane Tomkins (1828–1887), were serving as medical missionaries. William Tydeman, born in Suffolk, studied medicine under Drs. Thomas MacKern and Joseph Kidd at the Royal Homeopathic Hospital in London.

Edith's maternal grandparents were in Jamaica for about twenty years. Around 1867, they moved permanently to the United States, settling first in Asheville, North Carolina, where William Tydeman opened a medical practice. Their daughter Emily Fannie was born there in 1870. In 1872, the family relocated to Knoxville and lived first on Prince Street (now Market Street), according to the 1880 U.S. Census. City directories for the next ten years show the Tydeman residence and physician's office at 109 Vine Street.

In 1886, young Dr. Douglas Caulkins (1858–1936) joined the practice, which became known as Tydeman & Caulkins. Douglas Caulkins was born in New York, came to Knoxville at age thirteen, taught school at seventeen and studied medicine in Athens, Tennessee (1879–80). In 1881, he was elected principal of Bell House School, at the corner of State and Main in downtown Knoxville.[34] He attended Rush Medical College in Chicago (1882–83), then earned his homeopathic medical degree from Hahnemann Medical College in Philadelphia in 1885. Douglas was also on staff at Knoxville General Hospital and frequently gave his services to St. John's Church Home, an orphanage on Linden Avenue in East Knoxville. This brick home, built in 1890, is where up to forty children were housed. Lucy and Douglas married in 1886, and Edith was born the following January.

By 1900, the Tydemans and Caulkins were living and practicing medicine at 503 Vine Avenue just west of Immaculate Conception Church. Lucy's younger sister Emily Fannie took a premedical course at South Carolina College at Columbia (1896–98). William Tydeman, seventy-four, died on January 22, 1898, in Columbia.[35] Due to failing health, he had spent the last four years of his life alternating between South Carolina in the winter and North Carolina in the summer.[36] Douglas took over the medical practice. In 1901, Emily earned a degree in homeopathic medicine from Southern Homeopathic Medical College in Baltimore, Maryland. She practiced there for thirty-four years and then retired to Southern Pines, North Carolina, the state of her birth, where she died in 1945.

Edith graduated from the University of Tennessee in 1908, taught school for a year and then became a stenographer. A large number of women in the business workforce had previously taught school but found the wages inadequate. By 1915, more than half of all clerical workers were women. Many young women in Knoxville attended Draughon's Practical Business College, one of thirty Draughon's Colleges in the Southeast. An ad in the May 22, 1909 *Knoxville Sentinel* boasted that 75 percent of U.S. court reporters used the system of shorthand taught at Draughon's. The college also taught typewriting, telegraphy, bookkeeping, commercial banking and business law.

According to Knoxville city directories, Edith worked eight years for the Knoxville Railway and Light Company (KR&L), one of, if not the largest, employers in the city at the time. In 1905, Knoxville's four major electric and transit companies—Knoxville Gas Light Company (organized in 1840), Knoxville Gas Company (1903), Knoxville Electric Light and Power Company (1888) and Knoxville Traction Company (1898)—were consolidated as KR&L. By 1910, the city had forty-two miles of streetcar track carrying eleven million passengers per year. Did Edith attend Draughon's after finishing at UTK? We don't know. And we don't know if she was a

Edith Caulkins, "Gay Street, 1900–1910." *Library of Congress, Detroit Publishing Company.*

stenographer for one of KR&L's executives, but given her education, it is likely. But we do know, based on the accompanying 1910 photo, what Gay Street looked like as she walked or rode a streetcar to the KR&L offices in the 600 block.

In late June or early July 1914, Edith and her mother visited Jamaica, taking advantage of the reduced summer fare of $150 and sailing on the SS *Santa Marta* from New York to Kingston. The *Santa Marta* was a "banana boat," a beautiful vessel updated to accommodate the growing number of tourists seeking tropical climes. Built for United Fruit Steamship Company, under the British flag in 1909, the *Santa Marta* served the New York–Jamaica–Cuba–Central America route. In 1914, because of relaxed navigation laws, the British Union Jack was replaced with the Stars and Stripes.

Known as the Great White Fleet, these refrigerated cargo steamships could carry about one hundred passengers and several thousand stalks of bananas. Painted white, they resembled yachts, but the color kept the temperature of the bananas down by reflecting the tropical sun. UFC brochures claimed that its fleet was "unparalleled for the excellence of accommodation." The "lounge," or "social room," on each ship had a piano and a music cabinet containing a large selection of recorded music, plus a library of books, magazines and newspapers in several languages. There were mahogany-paneled smoking rooms, lobbies fitted as sitting rooms and a ninety-seat dining room. A few of the cabins had private baths, but most had only a sink. Shared bathing and toilet facilities along the hallways were the norm in all but the largest oceangoing passenger vessels in the first decade of the twentieth century.

Jamaica had just begun to see an economic boost from tourism and was being touted as the "new Riviera." It was anticipating the opening of the Panama Canal in early August 1914. The island must have looked very different than the one Lucy had experienced as a child fifty years before. The timing of the mother-daughter trip was fortuitous. They arrived back in New York on July 25, three days before Austria-Hungary declared war on Serbia, officially starting World War I. On August 4, Britain declared war on Germany. Jamaica was a British colony and, although far from the battlefront, was the only Caribbean colony to have a permanent imperial garrison, with a battalion of the original West India Regiment stationed on the island. As soon as war was declared, the whole island economy was diverted from catering to tourists to training and supplying troops and preparing for possible invasion. About ten thousand Jamaicans enlisted.

Sadly, Edith died four years later, on September 18, 1918. Her death certificate lists the cause of death as typhoid fever, but we wonder if she didn't actually die of the Spanish flu. Symptoms in 1918 were so unusual that, initially, influenza was misdiagnosed as dengue, cholera or typhoid. Spanish flu cases were documented in Nashville and Johnson City in early September. In Knoxville, the numbers mounted rapidly. By October 5, the City of Knoxville had 200 confirmed cases of Spanish flu, not counting those involving the students at the University of Tennessee nor the hundreds of troops training on campus as part of a new government program called the Students' Army Training Corps.[37] By the end of November, there were 131 deaths and 8,984 cases. Most patients were between twenty-one and forty years old.

> [Dr. William R. Cochrane] *had been appointed secretary of the city's Board of Health. It was a part-time job, but it made him Knoxville's leading medical authority....On Sept. 29, Dr. Cochrane said, "Any intelligent physician knows that the Spanish Flu, which has caused so much excitement lately, is a form of la Grippe. Here in Knoxville we have no serious cases reported, and although the number of cases will probably grow for the next week or so, I do not think there is any cause for alarm." By the end of that next week, Dr. Cochrane had changed his mind.*[38]

Edith did not live to see the signing of the armistice on November 11, 1918. Like her aunt Emily, Edith never married. In 1929, the Edith Caulkins Memorial Dormitory was opened and dedicated at St. John's Church Home. Lucy, until her death in 1949, continued to live on Vine

Avenue with her daughter Lucile; Lucile's husband, John Chaffin; and their son John Jr.

Also buried in Old Gray are Edith's grandparents William Watson and Letitia Jane Tydeman; her parents, Douglas and Lucy Caulkins; her sisters Marion Caulkins Jackson McNabb and Lucile Caulkins Chaffin; and her aunt Emily Fannie Tydeman.

VIRGINIA ROSALIE MICHIE COXE

The tombstone of Virginia Rosalie Coxe (1863–1906), poet and novelist and author of *The Embassy Ball*, is memorialized with verse and one of Old Gray's most beautiful statues. Virginia was born in Virginia and educated in Georgia, where she met her future husband, Joseph Carson Coxe (1854–1923). They married in 1882 in Atlanta and lived variously in New Jersey, Spain, Georgia and North and South Carolina before settling in Knoxville. Coxe was a descendant of the McDowell/Coxe family, owners of Green River Plantation in Rutherfordton in western North Carolina. He made his wealth from Pennsylvania coal.

Virginia Rosalie Coxe. "Mrs. Joseph Carson Coxe, American Novelist." Illustrated American, *New York, Jun 3, 1898, photo by Dupont, page 613.*

In Knoxville, the couple lived at Crescent Bluff on Kingston Pike, an elegant mansion with an Italian rose garden overlooking the Tennessee River. *Leslie's Weekly* of April 1900 described the Coxe estate as "a beautiful country seat just west of Knoxville where Mrs. Coxe entertains her friends in sumptuous fashion." A notable event of the 1900 Knoxville season was a visit by the New York poet Ella Wheeler Wilcox to Crescent Bluff and the series of socials hosted by the Coxes that followed, culminating in a reception at the Women's Building at Chilhowee Park.

Virginia had other talents besides writing—she was a musician, a gardener and, in 1903, was granted a patent for a card game. In 1901, she was given consent to publish a new novel, *House of Folly.*[39]

The Coxes had two children, both born in Atlanta: Annie Eleanor (1882–1896) and Virginia Rosalie (1882–1978). In November 1905, Virginia

Rosalie, the surviving daughter, married Nathaniel (or Daniel) Baldwin Hull of the Savannah cotton Hulls. The wedding, in St. John's Episcopal Church in Knoxville, was described as "one of the most magnificent in recent times."

Virginia Rosalie Coxe died the following June at age forty-three. The death certificate lists the cause as Bright's disease, a historical term for a group of kidney diseases. In modern medical terms, the condition is described as acute or chronic nephritis. A notice of her death in the *New York Tribune* of June 25, 1906, was brief: "Virginia Rosalie Coxe, an author and the wife of an eccentric coal mine owner of the Pittsburgh section, is dead." Joseph never remarried and lived the last sixteen years of his life in Rome. He was a frequent traveling companion of the Knoxville Audigiers. He died of pneumonia while in Lucerne, Switzerland, in 1923 and is buried in Old Gray.[40]

Crescent Bluff burned in 1911 and was rebuilt in 1915. The new two-story Neoclassical-style house was designed by architect John Russell Pope (1874–1937) for Hanson Lee Dulin. Pope is best known for the National Gallery of Art in Washington, D.C. From 1961 until the mid-1980s, the Dulin home was known as the Dulin Art Gallery. From 1987 to the present, it has been a private residence.

As for Virginia Rosalie's writing career, she published a few poems and short stories in magazines but was best known for her 1897 novel *The Embassy Ball*.[41] A review of the novel appeared in the *New York World* on March 5, 1898.

> *It is a new society which Virginia Rosalie describes—a most remarkable society. There is about it a photographic faithfulness and detail which would suggest a personal association with the truly great people who are the characters. The book may be taken as a guide to what is said and done in this high world, according to the gospel of Virginia Rosalie. The characters are aristocrats. The men are usually "lazily puffing Perfectos," drink only "the amber foaming liquid," which may mean Scotch whiskey and soda or champagne, and the high-priced wines familiar on the cards of fashionable cafes. There isn't much of a plot to the story, and it doesn't need a plot.... The conversation is so brilliant and the French so humorous that one doesn't miss the plot.*

Frank Leslie's Popular Monthly, whose editor was actually Mrs. Frank Leslie, gave a more positive review in its January–June 1898 edition.

Virginia Rosalie Coxe. *Dingee Guide to Rose Culture: 1850–1910*; Dingee & Conard Co.; Henry G. Gilbert Nursery and Seed Trade Catalog Collection; Wikimedia Commons.

One of the insistent demands made upon fiction is that it must amuse and entertain.…In The Embassy Ball, Virginia Rosalie Coxe satisfies those requirements and has fulfilled another as well—that of portraying scenes and characters with which she is familiar and in a way that leaves little to be desired. The story sparkles with life and vivacity, and is replete with epigrammatic sayings.…This book of Mrs. Coxe's can be described in no more terse and true way than by calling it an "up-to-date" society novel, and it leads one to expect that she will do still better work in the future.

We don't know how well the novel sold, but, as still holds true today, a critic's view does not always predict a book's popularity with the masses. Virginia was popular enough in 1900 for a new rose to be named for her. The rose, a brilliant red hybrid tea rose, was introduced in Germany by the famous rosarian Peter Lambert. Sole rights were conveyed to the Dingee & Conard Company of West Grove, Pennsylvania, the foremost rose grower in the United States at the time. The company named it in honor of Virginia Rosalie Coxe "whose success as a writer has brought her prominently before the public."

Virginia's father, John W. Michie (1825–1898), is also buried in Old Gray.

CHARLES HUFF DAVIS

Charles Huff Davis.
Findagrave.com.

Charles Davis (1875–1918) was born in Lebanon, Virginia. Not long after, his family moved to Knoxville, where he attended city schools and then Baker-Himel School, a college preparatory school for boys. In 1894, he graduated from the University of Tennessee and for a time was undecided about a career. In 1895–96, he worked as a journalist, writing a society column for the *Knoxville Tribune* under the pseudonym Jim Holmes. His clever style of writing made him a hit with the locals, especially his back-and-forth barbs with "Girl about Town," an anonymous columnist who had moved from Chattanooga. The sparring wordsmiths were the man of traditional values versus the progressive woman, long before Tracy and Hepburn. "Girl about Town" was Lilian Hickman Warner, who had followed her journalist husband, Lorenzo "Lon" Warner, to Knoxville from Chattanooga, where they had both worked for the *Chattanooga News*.

A clue to how Charles found his life's work may be in an 1896 Holmes column. He recounted running into a woman he hadn't seen in a while, a woman whom he had "felt interested in for a considerable length of time." He asked what she was employing herself with, and "she replied that she was learning to be useful."[42] Charles must have given the lady's comment considerable thought, because not long after he entered the University of Tennessee College of Medicine. He graduated in 1898, and his address at the graduation banquet on March 29 was titled "The Profession We Have Chosen." After choosing the specialty of eye, ear, nose and throat, he graduated from the Chicago Eye and Ear College in 1899 and was immediately appointed senior intern at the Illinois Charitable Eye and Ear Infirmary in Chicago. In 1901, he moved to Knoxville to be near his parents in Jonesboro and opened his practice in the Empire Building, on the corner of Church Avenue and Prince (now Market) Street.

In 1902, Hortense Burton (1878–1959) of Applethwaite, Christiansburg, Virginia, at the suggestion of an aunt and uncle who lived in Knoxville, came to Dr. Davis for treatment. She was in town for several months, making friends and participating in the Hospital Bazaar of December 12 and 13, 1901. The two-day bazaar, held to raise money for a new hospital, was in the armory hall and, in addition to several themed booths, included a midway, restaurant, performances by the university glee club and a ragtime band, a cake walk and an evening dance. Hortense and two other young ladies portrayed fortune tellers in the Booth of Ishmaelia.[43]

Hortense returned to Virginia on August 29, 1902. At some point during her ten months in Knoxville, a romance had ensued, and on Thursday, October 2, 1902, the *Journal and Tribune* noted that Dr. Charles Huff Davis had spent a delightful three weeks in Christiansburg, Virginia. Charles and Hortense were married on June 25, 1903, in a quiet ceremony at her home in Virginia.[44] After a week visiting friends in Virginia and Bristol, Tennessee, the couple was at home with Davis's parents on Luttrell Street in Knoxville. That same year, Charles was elected secretary of the Knox County Medical Society.

Charles had already begun making himself useful. For many years, he performed free surgeries for St. John's Orphanage and was a specialist on call with the Child's Free Clinic in Knoxville, which provided free treatment to indigent children. In 1906, the Davises moved to a fine home on Laurel Avenue and were often in the society pages, particularly Charles, who was a popular speaker and a fine tenor. He performed with the Methodist and Episcopal choirs, often solo, was a frequent toastmaster at his annual medical fraternity gathering, was always a speaker at the annual medical association meetings in various eastern cities and gave free lectures to Knoxville groups such as the YMCA and the Womens' Anti-TB League. In 1908, he joined the medical staff of Knoxville General Hospital and in 1913 was elected treasurer.

In October 1918, the influenza epidemic arrived in Knoxville. Called the worst disaster in the history of Tennessee, it swept over the state in the last months of 1918 and continued in some parts of the state through the first four months of 1919.[45] There were over 1,600 influenza cases in Knoxville and more than 70 deaths, and from September 15, 1919, to December 30, 1919, more than 9,000 deaths due to influenza and pneumonia were recorded by the Tennessee State Board of Health. In March 1918, Hortense volunteered to work at the Red Cross station over the Market house and was made director of surgical dressings, which were sent to American soldiers in France. In October, she contracted the flu and had to resign her position but recovered. Charles also contracted the flu as well as pneumonia but did not survive. Shortly before his death on October 23, two months shy of his forty-third birthday, he told his attending physician to seek a cure for the flu. Due to the epidemic, he requested that his funeral be private.[46] In March

1919, the Knox County Medical Association adopted a memorial resolution in honor of Dr. Charles Huff Davis: "He was a man of forceful character, cheerful disposition, a staunch and loyal friend of organized and scientific medicine. His aid and counsel were always on the side of progress toward the cure or relief of humanity....He was a man, young, at the zenith of his profession who loved to live because life was full of pleasure, of possibilities, yet he feared not to die."

Hortense remarried in Manhattan in 1922 to Charles Sharp Grant (1888–1948) and moved to Ghent, Norfolk, Virginia. She drowned in October 1959 in "the waters of the Hague." The community of Ghent, near the Hague Inlet, was founded by two Dutchmen. Today, the Hague is still prone to tidal flooding.

An interesting remembrance of Dr. Davis appeared in the October 19, 1936 *Knoxville Journal*. The article was a plea for donations to the Knoxville Association of the Blind and profiled a blind woman named Rosa Byous employed in the association's workshop. Byous, forty-seven, was born on a farm in Jefferson County, moved to Knoxville at age three and caught measles at nine. She began gradually losing her sight and from the age of fifteen until age thirty was treated by Dr. Davis at the free clinic in an attempt to slow the inevitable loss of vision. She said the last thing she remembered being able to read was the notice of Dr. Davis's death. Soon after he died, ending her treatment, she went completely blind.

PEREZ AND SUSAN PENNIMAN DICKINSON

Cemeteries are full of sad love stories. One of Old Gray's saddest involves Perez Dickinson of Island Home Farm fame. Perez was born in 1813 in New Braintree, Massachusetts. He spent two years at Amherst College and, in 1829, came to Knoxville,

> *where his brother-in-law, Joseph Estabrook, was principal of the Knoxville Female Academy. Dickinson was penniless when he arrived in Knoxville but was highly motivated to achieve success. He taught at Hampden-Sydney boys' school his first year, then attended UT (then East Tennessee College) and was awarded an honorary AB degree in 1830.*
>
> *After graduation he entered a business partnership with James Cowan leading to the formation [in 1858] of an enduring grocery and dry goods*

wholesale business, Cowan, McClung, and Dickinson. Dickinson also served as President of First National Bank, and according to French Broad-Holston Country: A History of Knox County Tennessee (East Tennessee Historical Society, 1946), "its stockholders were always paid in gold as long as Dickinson was President."

He bought a lot on [the corner of] *Main* [and Locust] *Street*[s] *and built for himself and his mother* [Lucinda Foster Dickinson, (1789–1855)], *a mansion with wide and spacious rooms, broad porches, and cellars.*[47]

The house, built in 1831, was demolished around 1950 and is presently the site of Bank of America.

An article about this love story appeared in the February 25, 1900 *Knoxville Journal & Tribune* and included a brief mention of the marriage: "In 1945 Perez decided he needed a wife and went back to his hometown, New Braintree, in search of one. He married Susan Penniman there that same year and brought her home to Knoxville."[48]

They married in April in Amherst. Perez was thirty-two, and Susan was twenty-two. The marriage may not have been as hasty as the article implied and was likely preceded by a lively correspondence. The Dickinsons and Pennimans knew one another. Emily Dickinson, Perez's cousin, had been one of the first two music students of Susan Penniman's sister-in-law Eliza Houghton Penniman (1822–1903), according to Eliza's 1900 diary.[49] The Houghtons had moved to Amherst in 1835, and sixteen-year-old Eliza began teaching instrumental and vocal music in her home. Eliza continued her own musical education at Amherst Female Seminary and, between 1839 and 1840, at Amherst Academy, where Emily began in 1840. Both names are in the 1840–41 Amherst Academy catalog. Eliza married Susan's younger brother, veterinarian Dr. James Penniman, in Amherst in 1846.

Back in Knoxville, Perez and Susan continued to live in Dickinson's much-admired house on Main Street. They took frequent carriage rides in the surrounding countryside, and Susan, a nature lover who had lived on a farm in her youth and who had fond memories of gathering flowers and roaming the fields as a girl, expressed her wish to live in the country. "She had loved the forest land by the river, and had wished for a white country house with large rooms for entertaining relatives and friends."[50] Susan, like Perez's cousin Emily, was likely influenced by the Concord Transcendentalists, who revered nature as a source of beauty, physical and spiritual insights and sanctuary. The transcendentalist movement spanned the girls' formative years (1836–47). Ralph Waldo Emerson's seminal essay "Nature," published in 1836, presented the transcendentalist philosophy, and the journal the *Dial*, published in Boston in 1940–44, created a vehicle for their essays and reviews in philosophy and religion.

Perez promised Susan that he would buy her a farm and make it one of the finest in East Tennessee. Sadly, Susan never lived to see the Island Home farm Perez created in her memory. The couple had only four months together. An infant, Lucy Penniman Dickinson, was born on July 1, 1846. Susan died on August 9. Her obituary in the August 11 *Knoxville Standard* was brief: "Died—on Sunday the 9th instant, Mrs. S.P. Dickinson, consort of Mr. Perez Dickinson." (Before the Linotype machine was invented in 1886, every printed letter in the newspaper had to be set by hand, so obituaries were brief by necessity.) Baby Lucy died on October 13. Eliza Houghton and James Penniman were married on October 28. The Pennimans had two sons and three daughters, one of whom they named Lucy.

Perez never remarried. It is said that he never fully recovered. His mother, Lucinda, died in 1855, but he had many friends and was still inspired by the natural world.

> *He purchased the South Knoxville property in 1869, built the large Italianate house* [now part of the TN School for the Deaf campus] *there in 1875, and in subsequent years developed the land into a cattle farm. He next purchased Williams' Island* [now known as Dickinson's Island] *in the adjacent stretch of the TN River and named the farm "Island Home" after the island. The farm now had approximately 600 acres.*
>
> *Perez used Island Home as a summer cottage, a guest residence, and an agricultural and horticultural center. There he entertained local Knoxvillians and visiting dignitaries. He was very generous in opening the home to others and encouraged various civic groups and organizations to hold meetings at Island Home.*[51]

Perez invited church groups to hold picnics there and UT agriculture students to experiment with vegetable crops. His vegetables were said to be the first to arrive in the farmers market, but only to exhibit, not to sell. As much as he loved Island Home, he maintained his permanent residence on Main Street. He loved children and had several nieces and nephews nearby. He also loved seeing children in the Gay Street store. It is said he sent so many gifts to East Tennessee children at Christmas that he was called Santa Claus.

Perez retired from the wholesale firm in 1890. The 1900 *Journal & Tribune* article, published the year before his death, ends thus: "In 1898 Dickinson was advised by his physician to end his visits to the farm, and he rented it. It is still one of the finest [farms] in East TN and is a monument to the high ideals of scientific farming as held by the owner and moreover a tribute by him to one whose memory he ever cherished above all possessions." Perez Dickinson died at home on July 17, 1901, at age eighty-eight. At his bedside were many nieces, including great-nieces and grand-nieces. A lengthy and laudatory obituary appeared in the July 17 *Knoxville Sentinel*.[52]

DUCLOUX FAMILY

The Duclouxs were French Swiss members of Knox County's "Swiss Colony," founded in 1848, when Reverend Adrien Chavannes and his family settled on a 275-acre farm four miles north of Knoxville. These Swiss settlers arrived in Knoxville just before the railroad and saw the rowdy river town transform into a regional merchandising center before the Civil War. During the next sixty-five years, more than seventy-five families settled in the area, engaging in various agricultural and business pursuits. By the time of the Civil War, there were approximately twenty French-speaking Swiss families living in Knoxville.[53]

Most were members of the Open Brethren, a fundamentalist Christian group that had withdrawn from the National Protestant Church of Switzerland in 1824. They wanted more religious freedom than they had in Switzerland, and they were lured by promotions of eighteenth-century land developers George F. Gerding, a New York businessman, and Theodore de Cock of Antwerp, who formed the East Tennessee Colonization Company in 1844. The partnership purchased 170,000 acres of land in Morgan, Cumberland, White, Fentress and Scott Counties and offered it for pennies an acre in an effort to attract German and Swiss settlers to the area. After the Civil War, pamphleteers boasted of East Tennessee, with its ample farmland and temperate climate, as the "Switzerland of America":

Its towering mountains locking up deep, rich and verdant valleys and coves, its succession of ridges and valleys, its magnificent forests, its roaring streams, the general fertility of the soil, the glory of the climate, the salubrity of the atmosphere, the sublimity, beauty and picturesqueness of the scenery, the freshness and voluptuous abundance of the country, all conspire to make it one of the most desirable spots in America.[54]

The trip from Switzerland to Knoxville was an arduous two-and-a-half-month journey involving ships, trains, stagecoaches, steamboats and, finally, wagons. Initially, they settled in Wartburg, but finding the soil and market disappointing, they moved on, the German Swiss going to Gruetli-Laager and Hohenwald, Tennessee (the German *hohenwald* translates to "high forest"), and many of the French Swiss heading to the north and east parts of Knox County, in a square mile of wilderness called Grassy Valley (now Fountain City) and along Washington and Tazewell Pikes.

The Swiss immigrants were farmers, cheese- and winemakers, gardeners, teachers, ministers and government officials. *The Introduction to the Resources of Tennessee* by Joseph Killibrew, published in 1874, praised the Swiss settlers for their self-reliant character and strong work ethic; for their prosperous farms, which were models of efficiency, thrift and neatness; and for the sound improvements they made to the area. "Whatever work can accomplish they perform. They sell as much as possible and buy as little as possible. What they buy is the best. By the neighbors they are much respected. They make good citizens [and none among them] are idle croakers, dreaming of past glories."

Charles Ducloux (1836–1917) was born in Lausanne, a city on Lake Geneva, in the French-speaking region of Vaud, Switzerland. He arrived in Knoxville in 1856 and married Eliza "Lily" Esperandieu (1839–1874) in September 1859. Lily's father, Reverend Frederick Esperandieu, ran a French-English bilingual school in Knoxville and was a professor of French at East Tennessee University (1873–77). The Duclouxs had three daughters: Sophie Marie (1862–1944), Lucie (1866–1945) and Isabelle (1869–1945). Three Ducloux children died before the age of two: Alfred in 1861, Adele in 1872 and Fred in 1874. They are buried in Old Gray.

In 1863, Charles enlisted in the Confederate army as a private, fought in several battles in Tennessee and survived three bullets in 1864. After the war, he worked five years in New York before returning to Knoxville in 1872. He had a bookkeeping office on Gay Street and from 1885 to 1897 served as the Swiss consul in Knoxville.

Lily died at age thirty-five, and Charles never remarried. Sophie, the eldest daughter, never married and, after her two sisters married and left Tennessee, continued to live with her father until his death 1917. She was a French teacher in Knoxville public and private schools for many years

Lucie Francoise Ducloux Mercier.
Ancestry.com.

and was active in her community, including acting as treasurer of the East Tennessee Audubon Society (1911), volunteering in the Red Cross during World War I and serving on the executive board of the Conservation Exposition at Chilhowee in 1914. She also served as vice-president of the Nicholson Art League (1912), president (1913) and director (1916–17). Sophie and Isabelle traveled to Europe together at least twice. Ship passenger lists show them arriving in Glasgow in 1909 (visiting Lucie and Alfred)[55] and landing in France and Italy in 1933. Sophie died in 1944 at the family home on Laurel Avenue and is buried in Old Gray.

In 1902, Isabelle married James Alexander Dalziel, a native of Scotland who immigrated to America in 1895. They lived for a few years in Knoxville and then moved to Paso Robles, California. They had one child, Charles Dalziel, who was a Fulbright professor of electrical engineering and computer sciences at UC Berkeley for thirty-seven years. James died in San Diego in 1929 and is buried there. Isabelle died in Berkeley in 1945, and her body was brought back to Knoxville for burial in Old Gray.

Lucie studied art for several years in Europe and taught art in Knoxville before marrying. In 1898, she was one of the charter members of the Nicholson Art League. In 1899, she married Alfred Jules Mercier, a native of Scotland and a graduate of the University of Geneva, and they moved, first to Glasgow, Scotland, where Alfred had just been appointed French lecturer at St. Andrews University, and then in 1895 to Geneva, Switzerland, where he was professor of French language and literature at the University of Glasgow.[56] They had two daughters, Fleurance and Estelle. In 1906, after an eight-day voyage out of Glasgow, the Mercier family arrived in Knoxville for a three-week visit with Charles at the Ducloux residence on Fourth Avenue.[57] Lucie died in 1935 in Vevey, Switzerland, and is buried there.[58]

DUENNER FAMILY

The Duenner family is one of several Swiss German families buried in Old Gray. The Duenner children—Frederick Otto "Fritz" (1877–1905), Robert Henry (1883–1960), Aurelia Bertha (1885–1914) and Cecilia Elizabeth (1887–1979)—came of age during Reconstruction and the industrial age, when Knoxville was undergoing major growth and change. The postwar manufacturing boom brought thousands of immigrants to the city, and the population grew from about 5,000 in 1860 to 32,637 in 1900.

Their mother, Bertha Julia Aurin Duenner (1859–1894), and her parents were born in Germany. Their father, Robert Heinrich Duenner (1853–1898), and his parents were born in Switzerland. There was early sadness in the Duenner family. The first Duenner child, Robert Fritz, died in 1880 at the age of just two and a half months from a brain fever, a term used in the Victorian era for what is now known as encephalitis, an inflammation of the brain generally caused by a viral infection. Bertha died in childbirth in October 1894; the infant, Walter Aurin, died thirteen months later, in November 1895.

After Bertha's death, Robert Duenner, a traveling salesman, met Ella Young in Bakersfield, North Carolina, when he stayed at the Penland House (later the Young Hotel), where her parents were proprietors. They married in 1896, and Ella returned to Knoxville with him. He died two years later at age forty-five, leaving Ella to raise three stepchildren: Robert Henry (age eleven), Aurelia (nine) and Cecilia (seven). The eldest son, Fritz (twenty-one), a recent UT engineering graduate, was still living at home but was working as a draftsman with an engineering firm.

The Duenner sisters attended the Girls' High School on the corner of Union and Walnut Streets (space now occupied by the Daylight Building, which currently houses Union Avenue Books and the restaurant J.C. Holdway). The schoolhouse was a Gothic Revival building designed by architect Joseph Baumann. It was three stories tall with eleven classrooms. The Duenner brothers attended college; after high school, the sisters sought full-time employment.

Based on Aurelia's employment history, it is likely she attended one of several business schools operating in Knoxville at the time. With the growing number of merchants and manufacturers, there was a corresponding demand for clerical workers. Besides Draughon's Practical Business College, there was also McAllen Business and Shorthand College, Knoxville Business College, Clark's School of Telegraphy and Young School of Shorthand.

Some, like McAllen, offered both day and evening courses in shorthand, typewriting, bookkeeping, calculating machine operation and stencil cut.

As young working women, the sisters moved about quite a bit, in residence as well as employment. In 1904, Aurelia was a stenographer with the Southern Truck Company and was still living in the family home on Luttrell. By 1905, she was boarding at 807 North Fifth Avenue and was a stenographer with the *Knox Journal and Tribune*, which was under the editorship of William Rule. In 1906 and 1907, she and Cecilia were sharing a room in a boardinghouse on Church Street. Aurelia was a stenographer with Armour & Company, a subsidiary of the Chicago-based meatpacking manufacturer operating in the Old City, and Cecilia was a clerk with W.D. Kuhlman & Company, a drugstore on Gay Street.

Fritz left Knoxville around 1895, then, much like his father, went "on the road," spending six years living in hotels and boardinghouses in search of jobs in civil engineering. In 1903, at age twenty-eight, he married Willoughby "Willie" Bewley of Morristown. In 1905, the year Cecilia graduated from high school, Fritz died suddenly in Albuquerque, New Mexico, on his way to Mexico. His remains were shipped to Knoxville for burial in Old Gray.

Sometime in 1907, Aurelia met Charles Oliver Defibaugh (1885–1928), a Pennsylvania native working as a clerk in Bristol, Tennessee. They married on November 20, 1907, at Broad Street Methodist Church. The detailed wedding announcement closed with the following: "Mr. and Mrs. Defibaugh left at 10:30 pm for an extended honeymoon in the north. They will be at home to their many friends after December 20 in Bristol."[59] By 1910, the couple was boarding in Norton, Wise County, Virginia, and Charles was a cashier with the local Armour & Company. In 1913, they were living in Tampa, Florida, where Charles still worked as a cashier with Armour & Company. Sadly, Aurelia died in Tampa in 1914 at age twenty-nine, the cause of death unknown. Charles remarried in 1917 and died in Shreveport, Louisiana, at age forty-two.

Cecilia Duenner was in the 1905 Knoxville High School graduating class with director Clarence Brown. She was also in the Musical Club with Brown. Brown reproduced in detail a replica of their classroom for the film *Ah, Wilderness!*[60] On March 2, 1909, Cecilia married William Quail Johnston (1883–1964), a young pharmacist with Kuhlman. "Financial difficulties" at home had led Johnston to abandon early plans to become a physician, and he earned a BS degree in pharmaceutical chemistry from UT. In 1913, he and three fellow pharmacists pooled their money to open their own drugstore, Todd & Armistead Company. The Johnstons had three children and lived on Island Home Boulevard. In 1953, Johnston became the first pharmacist in UT history to be awarded the University of Tennessee Medical School's Golden T Certificate. He continued to work at Todd & Armistead until his death in 1964 at age seventy-two. Cecilia lived another fifteen years.

Robert Henry Duenner enjoyed a long and distinguished career as a surgeon in the U.S. Army. He graduated from George Washington University Medical School in 1910 and received his appointment to the U.S. Army Medical Corps in 1912. During World War I, he served in Honolulu, Hawaii, and with the American Expeditionary Forces, heading evacuation hospitals in France and Belgium. After the war, he served as trainer at several medical corps centers around the country, including Fort Sam Houston, Texas; Fort Knox, Kentucky; and Walter Reed Hospital. After retirement, he spent more than five years as medical director at the University of Delaware. Mentions of his achievements and visits to Knoxville to see Cecilia and her family appeared often in the *News Sentinel* society pages. He died in 1960 and is buried in Arlington National Cemetery.

JACOB EBAUGH FAMILY

If the predominant Old Gray story is the immigrant experience, it is because Knoxville, at the time the cemetery was founded, had a large population of foreign-born or second-generation Americans. The vast majority of America's early immigrants came from western and central Europe: Ireland, England, Wales, France, Scandinavia, the Netherlands and German-speaking areas. Their reasons for leaving their homelands were no different than those of immigrants today—they were fleeing intolerable, unsustainable conditions, sometimes abject poverty and oppression. Lured by the promise of land, employment and religious freedom, or simply by a utopian dream (as one nineteenth-century pamphlet read, "our East Tennessee, Switzerland of America, the garden spot of God's footstool"), they endured an often arduous ten-week journey in hope of a better life.

Immigration (halted briefly by the Civil War) peaked between 1820 and 1870. During that time, America went from being mainly a rural and agricultural society to the beginnings of an industrial one, attracting newcomers eager for opportunity. In the 1850s, Knoxville's prime employment opportunity was with the railroad. One of Old Gray's immigrant stories is the odyssey of the Ebaugh family, a segment of which began in 1752 and ended in Old Gray 127 years later.

Johannes Jacob Ybach was born in Bern, Switzerland, in 1731. The Ebaugh surname, originally spelled Ybach, is an example of how many foreign names acquired phonetic spellings once persons arrived in America. At age twenty, Johannes, supposedly the first Ebaugh in America,[61] sailed from Rotterdam on the passenger ship *Brothers* and landed in Pennsylvania on September 22, 1752. There was a "Jacob Ybach, Sen." also on board who may have been a relative. Not long after, probably early in 1753, Johannes married Anna Catherine Giess (born in Rhenish Palatinate, Germany, in 1731). The couple settled in Manchester, Carroll County, Maryland, where Johannes purchased one hundred acres and built a log home and a gristmill. They had thirteen children.

Jacob Ebaugh, son of Johannes's first son, Henry, married sixteen-year-old Rachel Reese, with whom he had ten children. After Rachel's death at forty, Jacob married Hannah Fetzer, who bore him four more. Jacob's second son, Benjamin Flowers Ebaugh (1810–1879), is the family patriarch and is buried in Old Gray. Benjamin moved around a bit before settling in Knoxville around 1840. He married Sarah Carnes (1826–1911) of Knox County in 1845 and worked many years for the East Tennessee, Virginia and Georgia Railway shops as a machinist. The Ebaughs lived on Crozier Street (now Central Avenue) near the area now known as Old City. They had seven children: Rachel, William, James Thomas, Benjamin, Margaret, Mary Frances and Emma.

The Ebaughs experienced the rapid expansion of Knoxville during the 1850s, an exciting time to be living near the railroad terminus downtown. In 1854, speculators donated land for Market Square. The first train rolled into town in 1855. By 1859, Knoxville had four hotels, at least seven factories, six churches, three newspapers, four banks and over forty-five stores. And between 1850 and 1860, the population grew from about two thousand to over five thousand.

From 1861 to 1865, the Civil War brought darker times. Benjamin, fifty-one, was too old to enlist, and his sons, by then railroad engineers, were legally exempt. Knoxville became "militarized"; about a dozen forts were built around the city, and a network of trenches was dug around its boundaries. The Ebaugh home, by then on Middlebrook Pike, was burned by Union soldiers.[62] Benjamin's daughter Margaret Ebaugh Parker (who lived to be ninety-nine years old) remembered the day a Union soldier came to the door and suggested the family take an outing for safety because of the possibility of fighting in the area. She was five or six at the time. She said that when the family returned they found their home in ashes. The city gave them refuge in the temporary military barracks in City Hall Park, which was then part of the campus of the Tennessee School for the Deaf on Summit Hill.

Benjamin didn't live to see the industrialization that brought rapid growth to Tennessee in the 1880s, but some of his children did. Daughter Rachel married John Hope, the son of well-known architect Thomas Hope, who designed Ramsey House, Statesview in west Knoxville and Rotherwood in Kingsport, Tennessee. John and his brother David began Hope Brothers Jewelers on Gay Street in 1864. During the Great Depression, the store, by then under the management of Hope grandsons, struggled and became Kimball's Jewelers in 1933. The Hopes lived in Fountain City and are buried in Greenwood Cemetery.

The other Ebaugh children, following their father's lead, were all involved with the railroad; James Thomas and Ben became locomotive engineers. Ben worked many years for the East Tennessee, Virginia and Georgia Railway. James worked for the Nashville, Chattanooga and St. Louis Railway for forty-three years and is buried in Nashville. Daughters Mary Frances and Margaret married engineers, and Emma married a boilermaker (one who builds and repairs locomotives).

Benjamin's obituary in the *Knoxville Daily Chronicle* states that he was "a man of peculiar turn and given to few words but [was] only known to be honored and respected."[63] Margaret, who died in 1956, was the last Ebaugh to be buried in Old Gray.

LIZZIE CROZIER FRENCH

Margaret Elizabeth "Lizzie" Crozier French (1851–1926) was a pioneering feminist who resisted and persisted until her death. She was one of Knoxville's leading intellectuals, a gifted essayist, lecturer, educator, social reform activist and, most famously, women's suffragist.

Lizzie was the daughter of Mary Williams and Colonel John Harvey Crozier. Colonel Crozier was also an attorney, a onetime U.S. congressman and Knoxville's first postmaster. The Crozier home was on the corner of Clinch and Gay, where the Farragut Building now stands. The home was known to have the finest library in the city. Lizzie was an avid reader long before she went away to school, first to the Georgetown Academy for Young Ladies at the Monastery of Visitation in D.C. (the first Catholic girls' school in America) and then to the Episcopal Female Institute in Columbia, Tennessee.

In May 1872, she married William Baxter French Jr., the cashier of the wholesaling giant Cowan, McClung and Company. William was the son of Knoxville lawyer William Baxter French Sr. and the grandson of Tennessee Supreme Court judge Hugh Lawson White. Lizzie's husband died suddenly eighteen months after the wedding, two days shy of his twenty-fifth birthday, leaving her with an infant son, William Williams French. Lizzie never remarried but soon found her vocation. In October 1885, she and her sisters, Mary Frazier Crozier and Lucy Graham Crozier, founded and directed the East Tennessee Female Institute. Lizzie emphasized public speaking and in 1887 published *A Manual of Elocution* for her students.

In the early 1890s, Lizzie performed popular recitations around East Tennessee as part of her activism. The February 19, 1891 *Johnson City Herald*, in its WTCU Notes column (Woman's Christian Temperance Union), stated, "Mrs. L. Crozier French, the State Organizer for East Tennessee, was enjoying a growing reputation as an elocutionist of rare attainments… with an ambition to employ her rare talents and accomplishments in some way that may aid the support of herself and [her] child."

In November 1885, Lizzie initiated the founding of the Ossoli Circle, the first women's club in Tennessee. It was to become the first club in the southern United States to join the General Federation of Women's Clubs. Lizzie was inspired to form the Ossoli Circle after having visited the Sorosis Women's Club in New York City. The Ossoli Circle is named for the early nineteenth-century transcendentalist and feminist Margaret Fuller Ossoli.

Lizzie closed the female institute in 1898 and devoted herself to women's rights. She founded the Women's Educational & Industrial Union and became the first woman to address the Knox City Council, when she stood up to demand the city hire a police matron to look after female jail inmates. The city had no one in line for the job. Lizzie filled in herself until a matron could be hired.

According to the April 2, 1902 *Birmingham Post-Herald*, Lizzie began editing a monthly journal, *The People*, "a journal of inquiry, protest and an exponent of the people." We can find no evidence that the publication ever made it into print, but this clipping in the Lizzie Crozier French Scrapbook (LCFS), McClung Collection, provides a more personal view of Lizzie's intellect, humor and activist zeal:

Mrs. L. Crozier French Edits Paper, p. 07
Contrary to the usual object of a woman's paper, the club organs, and those that discuss the fashions and other timely subjects which regale the readers of the woman's page in the daily papers, Mrs. French will make no effort to interest readers of this class.

In emphasizing her position, the editor says: "This publication claims not to be a guide to society ladies. It resigned all such ambitions to the Ladies' Home Journal and similar sheets. You will not learn from these columns how to butter your bread, or hold your fork. The best manner of folding your napkin will be left to your imagination. It will not undertake to instruct you in the number of the hairs of your head, nor the proper number of kisses you should give to your sweetheart. The editor of this journal takes it for granted that its readers are not inmates of institutions for the feeble minded.

In a somewhat lengthy editorial, Mrs. French left no doubt, however, as to the policy of The People. With her usual comprehensiveness and frankness she outlines the policy of her journal. "Education will occupy much space in The People, education in the highest and broadest sense of the word, including schools, the theatre, pleasures, ethical questions, health."

Mrs. French is particularly interested in municipal affairs of her own city. In an open letter, she has already challenged the "ring leaders," and she calls attention to certain municipal problems that will be discussed from time to time in her journal. Briefly the policy of The People is:

The People is not the propagander of any set of tenets, be they religious, political, philosophical or scientific. The People will investigate, as opportunity offers, any subject that is of vital interest to humanity, but will dogmatize about none. Great principles will be studied, and the endeavor will be to show how they may be made to govern the practical affairs of life. The policy will be to treat every subject with candor, but it is hoped with perfect good nature. The private character of no man or woman, nor their private affairs will be considered legitimate subjects for discussion in these columns. Public officials, together with all those, be they men or women, who are in professions that bring them before the public, will be dealt with as may seem fit from time to time, but neither flattery, nor spite will be permitted to dictate the spirit of any criticism. Institutions and people will stand on their own merit. The policy of The People will be controlled neither by fear, nor favor.

Further evidence of Lizzie's activist zeal continues on page two of the LCFS:

> *Mrs. French's aims will be to arouse the people of her city to certain conditions that now exist and she asks co-operation in the effort to rescue municipal and county affairs from the hands of the partisan politicians, be they Republicans or Democrats. She believes that for a people to allow partisans to manage their municipal and county affairs is to submit to be made victims of the spoils system. Mrs. French's journal, in other words is to be devoted to "the idealizing of the real and the realizing of the ideal." Among the pertinent questions asked by Mrs. French, and which may strike a responsive chord in many cities are the following: Why should the Sunday closing law be enforced against stores in general but not against barrooms? Why was the office of police matron abolished, after having been in successful operation for ten years? Abolished, notwithstanding the earnest protest of Knoxville's best citizens. Why is it that we have not enough money to make our public schools what they should be? Why is it that we have not even one little plat of ground for a resting place in the heat of summer? Why is it that the ordinances in regard to the keeping of our streets free of filth are not in any degree enforced? It is because the people have not organized. It is because the people have not said to the officials, "You must do your duty!" It is because the people have not said to the ring leaders, "Thus far shalt thou go and no farther." It is because the people have had no means of expressing their will.*

She was the first woman to address the Tennessee General Assembly and the Tennessee Bar Association. Her Tennessee Bar speech, "An Address on Women's Rights," became one of the most quoted speeches by suffrage groups. She traveled the country speaking and lobbying for equality. She told the crowd at one debate, "I wish I could say, 'Fellow citizens,' but since I am not accepted as a citizen by the government, I must say, 'Citizens and fellow servants.'" Folks said she inherited her father's oratorical brilliance.

French lived to see Tennessee ratify the Nineteenth Amendment and to cast her first vote. She died on May 14, 1926, a week after her seventy-fifth birthday, after suffering a heart attack during a visit to Washington, D.C., to lobby for a bill on behalf of working women. According to the *Journal Washington Bureau*, her death was attributed to "heart trouble complicated by a congestion of both lungs approaching pneumonia and by other physical ailments." Her son William, who lived in Birmingham, arrived three hours

Left: Lizzie Crozier French, Women's Suffrage Memorial. *Photo by Judy Loest.*

Opposite: Lillien Gaines monument. *Photo by Judy Loest.*

before her death. Her obituary stated that "she had a rare organizing ability and wisdom enough to see that ideals are not realized by dramatic strokes bringing immediate victories, but that they must be brought about by careful cultivation and education."[64]

In 2006, the City of Knoxville installed the Tennessee Woman Suffrage Memorial at Market Square downtown. The bronze sculpture honors the women who were leading campaigners for the state to ratify the Nineteenth Amendment to the U.S. Constitution to give women the right to vote: Elizabeth Avery Meriwether of Memphis, Lizzie Crozier French and Anne Dallas Dudley of Nashville. Lizzie is in the forefront. In 2021, Old Gray installed beside Lizzie's grave a commemorative plaque honoring her significant contributions to Knoxville and to women nationwide.

LILLIEN GAINES

The tombstone for little Lillien Gaines (1868–1876) has long been a favorite of Old Gray visitors. Over the years, secret admirers have left countless tokens of affection at Lillien's statue, including stuffed animals, coins,

flowers, bracelets, hair ribbons and dolls. What accounts for such heart-stirring interest? Perhaps it is the assumed approximation of the statue to the real Lillien. Or it may be the statue's pensive pose, or this inscription:

Sleep dear one and take your rest
We loved you dear
but Jesus loved you best

Or it may be a combination of all of these factors. Who was Lillien? We don't know much about her short life. In local newspapers, her name was most often spelled "Lillian." She was born on December 17, 1868, in Savannah, Georgia, to James Luttrell Gaines and Roberta Belle Porter, and she died on April 29, 1876, in Nashville, just four and a half months after her seventh birthday. The cause was cerebrospinal meningitis, a common and often fatal pediatric disease at the time. Vaccinations and antibiotics did not arrive until the 1940s. Water quality and sanitation were the major priorities in America's growing cities, but infrastructure was slow in coming. Installation of the first septic tanks did not begin until the 1950s.

Lillien's grandfather Matthew Gaines was the fifteenth mayor of Knoxville, the second of only two mayors to live in Blount Mansion. Her father, James, was born in Knoxville in 1839 and was a student in Chapel Hill, North Carolina, when the Civil War began. He joined the Confederacy, enlisting in the North Carolina Cavalry as a private and rose to the rank of colonel. He was wounded several times, and several horses were shot from under him. He lost his right arm at the Battle of Five Forks, southwest of Petersburg, Virginia, in April 1865.[65] He was engaged at the time to Roberta Belle Porter, a native of St. Charles, Missouri. One account says he offered to release her from their engagement due to his "mutilation and poverty." They were married on November 22, 1866, in Missouri and first lived in New York City, where James was a wholesale grocer. Their first child, James L. Gaines Jr., was born there a year later. Not long after, the family moved to Savannah, where Lillien was born. They then moved to Knoxville, where, for three or four years, James and his older brother Ambrose were engaged in the wholesale shoe business, Gaines & Bro. Company, Boots & Shoes, on the corner of Gay and Church Streets. James was elected Tennessee state comptroller in 1874, and the family moved to Nashville. In 1875, they moved to Chattanooga.

The first newspaper account of Lillien's condition appeared after her death in the *Knoxville Daily Tribune* of May 2, 1876:

At Gray Cemetery, yesterday afternoon, all that was mortal of Lillian, the bright and beautiful child of Colonel James L. Gaines, was laid away in the silent city of the dead to await the morning of the resurrection. The tidings of her decease received Sunday, cast a mantle of gloom over the hearts of a large circle of friends who had known and loved her. For while the character of her illness excited serious apprehension, yet anxious suspense had assumed the form of eager expectation that the hand of the death-angel would be averted. Affliction had laid its heavy hand upon her infancy, and every appliance that human skill could suggest had been tested to the uttermost in the effort to remove the physical infirmity which lay so heavily upon her buoyant life. When she was attacked by the disease which took her life, she had just been brought back from Indianapolis, where her case had been subjected to treatment, which it was fondly hoped would remove the impediment in her joyous childhood.

But "death loves a shining mark," and the beautiful and interesting child, whose brief existence was but the outpouring of rich and deep affections, has been called home ere she had learned the bitterness of human life.

Beautiful was she in life, and beautiful in death, for upon the calm, still features there shone the sweet serenity of peace, and there seemed a smile upon the lips unclouded by life's last agony, by which we know

That she was one beloved of God,
Made fairer even in death's icy sleep
  By the unwearied waking of the heart
  Which smiled as she went, beautiful, to Heaven.

The *Memphis Public Ledger* reported on May 3, 1876:

The friends of Comptroller Gaines in this city will be pained to learn that his little daughter, Lillian, died of meningitis Sunday morning, at his residence, in Nashville, after a lingering and distressing illness of many weeks. The remains were taken to Knoxville for interment.

James served three terms as state comptroller and in 1889 was elected third vice-president and general manager of the Tennessee division of the Tennessee Coal, Iron and Railroad Company. The third and last Gaines child, James L. Gaines Jr., was born in Nashville in 1878. James Sr. died there in 1910 and Belle in 1913. Their remains were returned to the family plot in Old Gray. Notable Gaines family members are buried there, including gallant Confederate officers (James and Ambrose), a mayor (Matthew) and a popular beauty (Ambrose's daughter Mary) who laid the first brick on Gay Street, the city's first brick street, in 1893. But it is little Lillien who stirs curiosity, imagination and affection.

HENRY R. GIBSON

Henry Richard Gibson (1837–1938) had a distinguished forty-year career in Tennessee politics, journalism and law, but the second half of his life was the most interesting. Born on Kent Island, Queen Anne's County, Maryland, on December 24, 1837, he graduated from Decker's Academy at Bladensburg in 1858 and from Hobart College in Geneva, New York, in 1862. On September 12, 1862, he married Margaret Frances "Fannie" Reed in Brooklyn. From March 1863 to July 1865, he served in the commissary department of the Union army and in September entered Albany (New York) Law School. He was admitted to the bar in December 1865 and commenced practice in Knoxville in January 1866. He moved to Jacksboro, Campbell County, Tennessee, in October 1866 and was appointed commissioner of claims by Governor William G. Brownlow two years later. His political career continued for eleven years as a delegate to the state constitutional convention (1870), a member of the state senate (1871–75) and a member of the state house of representatives (1875–77).

Gibson returned to Knoxville in 1876, founded the *Knoxville Republican* in 1879 and became its editor. He then became editor of the *Knoxville Daily Chronicle* in 1882. He served two years as U.S. pension agent at Knoxville and eight years as chancellor of the second chancery division of Tennessee (1886–94). He was professor of medical jurisprudence in the Tennessee Medical College (1889–1906) and authored *Gibson's Suits in Chancery* in 1891, now in its eighth edition and still used in UT's College of Law. During these years, he was in demand as a speaker, often presenting a series of law lectures at the YMCA. He was elected as a Republican to Congress (1895–1904) but declined to be a candidate for renomination in 1904. He retired from public life and moved to Washington, D.C.

These decisions may have been influenced by a traumatic experience. Representative Gibson was a passenger in the day coach on the eastbound train that wrecked in New Market, Tennessee, on Saturday, September 24, 1904. The crash killed at least 56 passengers and crew and injured 106. Gibson escaped with only bruised legs and a wrenched back and shoulder but witnessed gruesome scenes. "He and the other man whose name is not known were the only persons to escape alive from their demolished car. When he realized what had happened, Gibson found his legs pinioned fast but managed to extricate himself. One glance at the car showed it to be a mass of human beings, backs of car seats, grips, baskets, and wearing apparel of all sorts. There was not a sign of life except, near his side, a young man who had escaped death and was struggling to get out."[66]

Morally shaken by the horror, Gibson left a career in politics for one of writing Arthurian poetry. He moved away from East Tennessee and, in 1907, published a 368-page epic poem, *The Maid of Redenfayn: An Allegory of Two Worlds*. Comprising three books—"Loves and Dreams," "Ambition and Grief" and "Repentance and Joys"—the poem may have been an allegorical autobiography. In 1912, he published an expanded version of this poem under the title *The Ban of Baldurbane, an Epic*. These works received no mention in local newspapers beyond publisher ads, absent the author's name, offering the books for Christmas gifts for the price of one dollar each. These books can be read online at the Internet Archive.

Anticipating a lasting legacy, Gibson had the Old Gray obelisk erected in 1915. His first wife, Fannie, was buried there in 1918. He and Fannie had three children, two daughters and a son, Woolman, who died at age two in Jacksboro, Tennessee. Frances was also a published poet. Her poetry collection *The Moon Maiden and Other Poems* (1913) was favorably reviewed by the *New York Times* on January 11, 1914. She was a member and president of the Ossoli Circle and the Writers' Club, which frequently held meetings at the Gibsons' apartment in the Belles Truches flats[67] on Church and Henley Streets.

In 1907, at age seventy, Henry Gibson was consulting editor of the *American and English Encyclopedia of Law and Practice*; in 1918, at age eighty-one, he was associate reviser of the *Code of Tennessee*. In 1920, by then a resident of D.C., Gibson married a second time, to North Carolina native Elizabeth "Lizzie" Beckerdit, as reported by the *New York Post* on May 26. He was eighty-three; she was sixty.

Gibson was a favorite with the press in his later years, not simply because of his achievements and remarkable longevity but also because of his colorful and individualistic personality. In one of his last visits to Knoxville, in 1932, at age ninety-five, as guest of honor at the Lincoln Day Dinner, he traveled by train in his beloved skullcap and bathrobe and stayed at the Andrew Johnson, where the dinner was held. He reportedly spent most of his time there in bed and wore the same traveling attire to the dinner, which apparently made him appear somewhat regal. He received tributes from all the speakers and was described in news reports as venerable, slight but still virile.[68] Until the last year or so, bedridden, he continued to refuse all medicine, saying he was better off without it. When asked on his one hundredth birthday how one could attain that age, he replied, "Be yourself."[69]

Gibson died in D.C. on May 25, 1938, and his remains were cremated. It was never clear in obituary notices whether his ashes were actually deposited in Old Gray beneath the obelisk erected twenty-five years earlier. The May 27 *Knoxville News Sentinel* reported friends' uncertainty as to whether his ashes would be interred at Old Gray or scattered across his birthplace on Kent Island. According to the May 27 *Evening Star* of Washington, D.C., his funeral was held that day in the Hines Funeral Home with Reverend Harp of the Trinity Episcopal Church in Tacoma Park, Maryland, presiding. Burial was to be private. Lizzie died in 1943 in D.C. and is buried in the Congressional Cemetery.

One of Gibson's most formidable political acts was his dissent at the 1870 Tennessee state constitutional convention in Nashville opposing a provision that made a poll tax a prerequisite for voting. He declared the provision to be a privilege tax on what should be the freest right of Americans. Two days after Henry Gibson's death, a small editorial in the May 27, 1938 *Knoxville News Sentinel*, "Death of a Prophet," stated: "How prophetic was his attitude in that day. He foresaw clearly the abuses that would arise from this evil.... It is significant and, we hope, ominous that a man who denounced this evil in the beginning should be the last survivor of that convention, a lingering protest, as it were, against a provision that has led in these days to corruption of elections and the government itself."

JAMES ALEXANDER HENSON AND MARTHA CAROLINE BADGETT HENSON

The Henson vault is the most impressive in Old Gray, and for several years it was a point of pride for the city of Knoxville. The September 27, 1909 *Knoxville Journal and Tribune*, reporting on construction progress, called it the "handsomest mausoleum that has been erected in the state of Tennessee" and gave a detailed description of the structure:

> *The cripts* [sic] *will be made of fine Barre Vermont marble. The interior walls and ceiling will be of pink Tennessee marble highly polished, and the floor of the vestibule will be Venetian mosaic....The entire weight of the structure is 50,000 lbs. The monument is nearing completion and has been the object of labor for three months by five men under the direction of Mr. Adolph Geywitz of the Muldoon Monument Co in Louisville.*

The vault was Martha Henson's memorial to her husband, James Alexander "Alex" Henson (1847–1909). Henson "was a founder [along with

James A. Henson vault.
Photo by Judy Loest.

J.P. Haynes (1843–1904)] of the extremely successful Haynes-Henson Shoe Company and had far-reaching business assets."

> *In 1888* [the Hensons] *had been signers of the charter of St. John's English Lutheran Church, the first English-speaking Lutheran congregation in the city, and both were active members of the church. Church membership grew, and the congregation wished to build a church larger than the old Broad Street Methodist Episcopal Church building, which it had purchased in 1890. In 1910 Martha Henson donated a lot one block from the location of the church, and the church bought a second lot. Ground was broken for the church in 1911, and by the time the church was completed in 1913, Martha Henson had donated, as a memorial to her late husband, nearly $90,000 of the $100,000 cost of the Gothic Revival, architectural-style church designed by Knoxville architect R.F. Graf.*[70]

Haynes-Henson Shoes began in the early 1870s as a retail storefront at 509 Gay Street (about where Cruze Farm Ice Cream is today). The business enjoyed so much early success that the owners decided to go wholesale and, in 1886–88, built the Haynes-Henson Building at 312 Gay Street. The building miraculously escaped the Gay Street fire of 1897 and is now known as the Century Building. As early as 1906, Haynes-Henson was doing $1 million a year in business and soon became known as "Knoxville's Million Dollar Shoe House."

Martha (1850–1927) and Alex married on January 1, 1873, and lived for over a decade downtown on Prince Street (currently Market Street). The wholesale shoe business continued to grow, and in 1886, the Hensons bought and renovated the former home of Louis Gratz at 1030 Gratz Street in North Knoxville. Gratz, a lawyer, and Civil War veteran, was the first mayor of North Knoxville (elected in 1889). At that time, trolleys were still pulled by horses, and almost everyone in that community had a stable on their property. Electric streetcars would not come to Knoxville for another four or five years.

In 1908, Haynes-Henson relocated to the company's warehouse and showroom on Jackson Avenue in the Old City, now a residential building known as Jackson Ateliers. Alex Henson, after being an invalid for seven years due to paralysis, died the following year, and J.P. Haynes continued to run the business. When J.P. died in 1904, his son Frank took over. By 1916–17, sales had topped $2 million, and by 1920, the year of Frank Haynes's death, the firm had twenty-one salesmen covering ten states. That was the last good year, the end of the peak era of "Knoxville's Wholesale Row," and in 1930, Haynes-Henson was bought out by competitor Mountcastle-Hill Company, the South's largest mail-order house and wholesale shoes and clothing establishment.

After Alex's death, Martha personally managed her considerable financial holdings and was known as a quiet benefactress to many good causes. In 1910, she purchased two lots on Broadway and Central and deeded them for $1 to the trustees of St. John's English Lutheran Church in addition to $90,000 for the purpose of erecting a new church. Her will in 1927 left a bequest to UT in the amount of $200,000 for the construction of a girls' dormitory.

> *At the time Martha was the age to enter college, UT did not admit women. The building was designed by Barber & McMurry and cost $150,000. It had a capacity of 150 women (in double rooms) and provided a well-furnished reception room, ironing rooms, shower rooms, and a lounging room, where the residents were allowed to smoke and to play cards. Of considerable consternation, it had only one telephone. It had ice-water fountains on all floors. The rooms were furnished with maple furniture, and there were buzzers for each room.*[71]

Henson Hall housed Air Cadet Training Program students from 1943 until June 1944 but returned to housing women as soon as the program ended. It became an academic building in the late 1970s and today houses the College of Social Work.

Martha Henson died in 1927 and was interred in the Henson vault alongside her husband. The couple had no children. In 1928, Martha's bequest to the Lutheran Church for a boys' school was realized. The Williams-Henson Home and School for Boys opened on Maryville Pike with an initial enrollment of five boys.

ELIZA BOOND HODGSON

Old Gray serves as a reminder of how immigrants have shaped and enriched our city. Hundreds who came from France, Germany, Greece, Ireland, Italy, Switzerland and other nations are buried here. Eliza Hodgson (1810–1870) of Manchester, England, is one of the more intriguing because of her famous daughter, novelist Frances Hodgson Burnett, who wrote *The Secret Garden* and other novels. The world knows a lot about Burnett, but who was Eliza? What we do know is that, like most emigrants forced to leave their native land, she was both desperate and courageous in seeking a better life for her children.

When Eliza's husband, Edwin Hodgson, died of a stroke in 1853 at age thirty-eight, Eliza was thirty-nine and pregnant with their fifth child, Edwina. The other children were Herbert (eight), John (seven), Frances (four) and Mary (two). Until then, the Hodgsons had lived comfortably in a seven-room house, employed two maids and were prospering thanks to Edwin's business, a quality iron and brass home furnishings store. With his death, the family suddenly had no income. Eliza decided to try to run the business herself, but the Manchester economy, almost totally dependent on cotton for the textile industry, was crashing due to the American Civil War. She struggled for ten years, moving the family twice to subsequently smaller residences, the last backing up to a street of squalor and dire poverty. Diminishing returns eventually forced her to sell the business. Still, there wasn't enough to live on.

When a cheerful letter arrived from her brother William Boond asking her to come to Tennessee and offering employment to Herbert and George in his grocery and dry-goods business there, Eliza did not hesitate. On May 11, 1865, she and the four children (Herbert, now eighteen, had gone ahead weeks earlier) boarded the SS *Moravian* in Liverpool. It was the same day the Liverpool newspapers carried the news of Lincoln's assassination. After a three-week crossing to Quebec (cheaper than a direct crossing to New York), followed by a two-week train journey to Knoxville, William took them by wagon to his home in "Mill Row" in Mossy Creek (now Jefferson City), Tennessee, near the yarn factory where he worked as a finisher. When the factory soon failed due to the war-ravaged economy, he began a small business in Knoxville and moved Eliza and her children to a two-story log house in New Market, Tennessee, twenty-five miles east of Knoxville.[72]

New Market at the time consisted of a single unpaved street of modest wooden houses surrounded by forest and hills. At one end were a tannery and the Baptist church, at the other a blacksmith shop and the Methodist church. In the town center was a general store with postmaster, a couple of shoemakers, three churches, a carpenter, a brick mason and a saddler. Tennessee was lush and beautiful compared to Manchester with its coal smut and ashes, but the war had left the state ravaged—farmland lay barren, half-burned buildings still smelled of smoke, violence and theft abounded and homeless veteran amputees were everywhere. A year had passed since William's letter, and the postwar economy was dismal. William was able to employ Herbert in his store for a pittance and John at his gristmill for even less. If not for occasional provisions from sympathetic neighbors, the family would have starved that first winter.

Despite the family's reduced circumstances, Eliza attempted to re-create in their rustic cabin the life of a respectable Victorian family. The children were always properly dressed with shoes, stockings and good linen; and the dinner table, no matter how meager the fare, was always set with silver and napkins. The family, with their strange accent, education and genteel dress and customs, must have appeared odd in a community where luxuries were rare, especially a family in such obvious dire straits.

Frances, or Fannie, as she was known then, helped support the family with music lessons (they did have a fine piano) and began a Select Seminary for Young People in their home. For these she was often paid in provisions. The school soon failed, and Frances began writing seriously, picking and selling blackberries in the summer to buy paper and pencils. Rare glimpses into those early days were found in a special to the April 1, 1904 *Knoxville Sentinel* by Dandridge attorney Alexander Payne Hynds. Hynds was one of Frances's pupils in her little seminary.

A year later, William was forced to close his store, and the Hodgsons moved close to Knoxville in an even smaller house on a hilltop somewhere near present-day Knoxville College overlooking what is now the Mechanicsville neighborhood. Frances called the house Noah's Ark and from there continued to build her writing career. Herbert and George, now twenty-three and twenty-two, respectively, moved to town to find employment. Herbert found work at a jeweler's, where he learned to make and repair watches, a respectable trade. John, to Eliza's horror, became a bartender at Lamar House, now the Bistro at the Bijou.

By 1869, Frances, who had become quite the scribbler, was selling her stories to New York magazines, earning enough income for Eliza and her daughters to rent a run-down but comfortable rambling brick house in town above the river. The girls named it Vagabondia Castle and, as Knoxville began to resume its prewar role as a social and trading center, were able to enjoy the cultural life of the city. Eliza, weakened after a bout of flu or pneumonia, began a rapid decline. Her health was no doubt compromised by years of poverty and hard work but also decades in Manchester, the world's first industrial city, with a long and difficult history of urban air pollution. Eliza died in 1870 at age fifty-nine after only five years in America. Frances, who had become the primary wage earner, paid for her mother's burial in Old Gray.

Eliza lived long enough to imagine the possibility of a brighter future for most of her children. In just a few years, the sisters and Herbert married and left Knoxville: Herbert and his wife Ann Burnett (sister of Swan Burnett) to Norfolk, Virginia, where he became a respected organ builder; Frances and Swan Burnett to Paris for two years for his medical training and then to Washington, D.C.; Edwina and Frank Bridges first to San Francisco, where he taught music, and then to Santa Clara, California, where they became vintners; Mary Edith and Archer Fahnestock to New York. John, who drifted from bartending to odd jobs, became an alcoholic and died of spinal meningitis in a Knoxville hospital in 1904.[73][74] Frances paid for his burial in the same grave as Eliza but did not add a grave marker.

Most of what the world knows about Eliza, the woman, is in Frances's memoir, *The One I Knew the Best of All: A Memory of the Mind of a Child.*[75] Her "Mamma," she said, was not clever but obviously had other admirable qualities. "Only as long as she lived," wrote Frances:

> *her mind was like that of a kind, serious, young girl—with a sort of maidenly matronliness....She never was unkind or ungenerous because she was good to everything—even disreputable and objectionable stray cats and lost dogs brought in—with bursts of enthusiasm—for refuge....*[She]

never uttered a vulgarly sharp or spiteful, envious word or harbored an uncharitable thought—perhaps it was because of these things that one grew up knowing that her unspoken creed would be: "Be kind, my dear. Try not to be thoughtless of other people. Be very respectful to people who are old, and be polite to servants and good to people who are poor. Never be rude or vulgar. Remember to be always a little lady."

Frances is still beloved by many, but few know of Eliza. In November 2015, Eliza's great-great-granddaughter Penny Deupree and other Deupree family members visited Old Gray and placed a wreath on Eliza's grave. Today, only the wild violets decorate her tiny plot. Symbolic of modesty, violets seem a fitting decoration. Eliza is slipping even further into anonymity, but we need to remember her and other immigrants' stories. They remind us that anyone, even the most privileged, is a heartbeat away from illness or financial ruin; that, often, the only way out and up is through hard work and the generosity of others, and that most of us are here because America once welcomed a stranger.

The primary source for this section is Gretchen Holbrook Gerzina, *Frances Hodgson Burnett: The Unexpected Life of the Author of* The Secret Garden (Rutgers University Press, 2004).

RIDA MARIE JOUROLMON

Rida Jourolmon (1863–1930) was the daughter of Knoxville natives Minerva Stowe Baker and Joseph Henry Jourolmon. Joseph worked for the railroad, and the family lived at 719 Asylum Avenue. Rida's paternal uncle Leon Jourolmon was a prominent Knoxville attorney, and her only sibling, Henry Baker Jourolmon, was treasurer and, later, director of W.J. Thompson, publisher of *Gentlewoman Magazine*.

After graduation, Rida was a Knoxville educator for fourteen years, teaching at Hampden-Sidney School and the Girls' High School. On July 2, 1889, Rida was on her way to New York for a visit when the Norfolk & Western train she was riding in crashed near Thaxton, Virginia. In that horrific derailment, seventeen people were killed, twenty-one were injured and twenty-four were uninjured. Most of the casualties occurred in coach; Rida, luckily, was in a sleeper car and was among the uninjured. This disaster may have influenced her life's mission.

Rida Marie Jourolmon.
Ancestry.com.

In 1901, Rida took a leave of absence for a world tour, "hoping to benefit her health." Countries on her itinerary included England, France, Italy, Switzerland, Greece, Egypt, Beirut, Korea and China.[76] Accompanying others connected with the Presbyterian board of missions, she began teaching as a missionary in China. An online bio states: "Rida Jourolmon came to China in 1901 for her health, accompanying a friend returning to China. Having made herself efficient in the work of the Jiangyin Station, the station requested her appointment as a regular missionary. The appointment came in 1904, four years after she had been in China. She engaged in country work for women. She retired from active work in 1927."[77]

Jiangyin lies on the Yangtze River, about halfway between Shanghai and Nanking. There, where the river narrows the last time before entering its delta, were the military forts defending China's great waterway from invasion. The city manufactured cotton cloth extensively and was the market for a large population on both sides of the river.

The Presbyterian missionary work in Jiangyin began in 1895 with two academies, a woman's training home, a hospital and several chapels in city and country. By 1920, additions included a training school for nurses, separate high schools for girls and boys, a Bible school for women and a school for needy children. Interestingly, most female American missionaries had more freedom and power in China than they did in America. They worked primarily educating women and children. Chinese women lived isolated from society and were dominated by men. An 1843 article in the *Protestant Missionary Journal*, "Chinese Character," stated, "Confucian philosophy has done its best to unfit a Chinese for the possession of such a heritage, by assigning to woman nothing but the privilege of drudging for her lord." Only female missionaries could speak to Chinese women; thus, female missionaries, even though they had little influence on Chinese religion, did influence changes in Chinese culture regarding the rights of women.

Near the end of June 1911, Rida arrived in New York aboard the French liner SS *Chicago* out of Le Havre. She was on furlough, possibly to attend the wedding of her niece Lucille Jourolmon, who married Ernest Granby Dodds on August 30. She made other voyages back home to visit family and friends in Knoxville, North Carolina and New York and make reports to the Presbyterian Mission Society. She also usually gave talks at local organizations about China and her experiences there. In 1920, she spoke at Newcomer's Department Store, telling of Chinese customs and "methods of conducting mercantile shops" (an old Chinese proverb says, "A man without a smiling face must not open a shop") and, at the close, displayed several Chinese garments and explained the occasions for which they were worn.[78]

In 1927, the National Revolutionary Army launched a communist purge in Nanking, known as the Nanking Uprising. Both nationalist and communist soldiers within the NRA participated in the rioting and looting of foreign-owned property, and the Chinese government forced missionaries to leave for their safety. The *Knoxville News Sentinel* reported that Jourolmon was "witnessing the horrors of the Chinese civil war."

A May 13, 1927 article in the *News Sentinel* described their harrowing flight out of China:

> *Late one evening the missionaries received a message by radio to flee to Shanghai. Within two hours afterwards the mission buildings were entered by the Chinese and their contents destroyed....* [The missionaries] *divided into two groups, which were to take different routes to a point where a boat would take them into Shanghai. All night long they walked, fearful of meeting soldiers, but arrived unharmed. The second party...were held up by two soldiers* [and] *relieved of all personal belongings including watches, rings, and even glasses but no harm was done them. After getting on the boat, the mission workers could hear bullets pattering against their boat.... The boatmen in their haste ran onto a sandbar and were compelled to remain there during the night until the tide came in and lifted the boat.*

Ocean liner passenger lists for April 1927 show that Rida returned to the United States aboard the *Empress of Canada* from Shanghai to Seattle. Soon after her return, she moved to Montreat, North Carolina. Montreat (a combination of the words *mountain* and *retreat*) was for many years the conference headquarters for the Southern Presbyterian denomination. It was also a retreat center for Presbyterian missionaries on furlough, and many retired there. In November, she told reporters that she had not been allowed to bring any personal possessions with her out of China and that one missionary had been killed.

Jiangyin Station was totally destroyed in 1937 when the Japanese Imperial Army launched a full-scale invasion and brutal massacre known as the Rape of Nanking. Although approximately three hundred thousand Chinese were killed, there were still Presbyterian and other Western denomination missionaries in the area, and they created a Safety Zone, which sheltered several hundred thousand refugees.

Rida died at Montreat on November 22, 1930. She is buried with her parents in Old Gray. Her brother Henry died in 1933 in Manhattan; his cremains are in Fresh Pond Crematory in Mount Crescent, Queens, New York.

THOMAS W. KELLER

Often, an Old Gray surname is the same as that of a famous person, and it sparks one's curiosity: "Could this person be a relative?" There is a greater chance of this being the case, given that Old Gray was founded in 1850, when the U.S. population was just 23.2 million (today, it is 331.9 million), so the branches of a family tree did not have a long reach. The Old Gray tombstone for Thomas W. Keller (1852–1916) brings up the question, "Was Thomas related to Helen Keller (1880–1968)?" It turns out that, yes, Thomas and Helen were first cousins. Thomas's father was Francis "Frank" Foreman Keller (1816–1901), the older brother of Helen's father, Arthur Henley Keller (1836–1896).

The Kellers originated in Zurich, Switzerland, with Hans Cunrath "Conrad" and Barbara Glaar Keller. Sometime between their marriage in 1728 and the birth of their first child, Casper Keller, in 1736, the Kellers immigrated to America, settling first in Pennsylvania. By 1740, the family had relocated to Frederick County, Maryland, where Casper's son David Keller was born in 1788. In 1813, David married Mary Moore of Rockbridge County, Virginia. Mary's father, Colonel Alexander Moore, was an aide to General Marquis de Lafayette at the surrender of Yorktown, and she was a second cousin of General Robert E. Lee. The Moore family comprised wealthy planters of Virginia. They trace their lineage to Sir Thomas Moore of England and were among the first settlers in Virginia.

David and Mary moved to Knox County, where David entered the mercantile business, hauling his goods in wagons or on horseback twice a year from Philadelphia. In 1820, David and his family moved to Alabama, locating near Tuscumbia, where he remained until his death. Their first two children, Alexander and Francis Foreman "Frank," were born in Knox County before the relocation; the other seven children, including Helen's father, Arthur Henley Keller, were all born in Tuscumbia.

Arthur Keller studied law at the University of Virginia, served as a captain in the Confederate army and later purchased and became editor of the *Alabamian* in Tuscumbia. He had two sons by his first wife, Sarah Rosser, and after her death he had two daughters with his second wife, Kate Adams, the first of whom was Helen, born in Tuscumbia in 1880.

Frank married Mary Ann Crozier, and they had seven children, the sixth of whom was Thomas Wells Keller. Both Frank and Thomas were born in Knox County on the family farm at what was then called Keller's Bend. The nearest settlement at the time was Campbell's Station (modern-day Farragut). Thomas and his wife, Laura Lackey, were married in 1872, and they had seven children and lived first in Louisville, Tennessee, then at 221 West Fifth Avenue, which was sold two years later for the construction of the new Christian church. The remainder of their married life was spent at 1800 West Clinch Avenue, when Thomas worked first in the railroad construction contracting business and, later, often with his brother Robert, in Knoxville real estate.

In 1889, Helen, nine, and her teacher, Annie Sullivan, first visited the Keller family in Knoxville.[79] In later years, Helen visited when in the area on lecture tours. In September 1913, Helen was the guest speaker at the National Conservation Exposition at Chilhowee Park in Knoxville. The August 2 and 13, 1913 *Knoxville News Sentinel*, announcing her upcoming visit, reported that while in Knoxville she would be "entertained by her kinspeople" and that "Mr. and Mrs. T.W. Keller have visited her while in New York several times." On Helen Keller Day at the exposition, "The Kellers had special reserved seats at the auditorium, and following the exercises, went up and met the speakers. The Knoxville Kellers presented Miss Helen Keller with a very large and handsome bouquet of roses at the close of her talk."[80] Helen Keller Day drew nearly eighteen thousand visitors, and the standing ovation was so long that Helen spoke briefly a second time. Thomas was sixty at the time and an active leader in the Knox County Civic Federation and was founder and elder of First Cumberland Presbyterian Church. Helen was thirty-three.

Thomas died suddenly on March 16, 1916, succumbing to a heart attack while attending an annual session of the Presbytery in Maryville, Tennessee.[81] Helen had been in Knoxville only a few weeks before, delivering a lecture at the Bijou Theater on February 26 under the auspices of the United Daughters of the Confederacy, but it is not known if her cousin was in attendance. Her name appeared frequently in Knoxville newspapers for another fifty years.

Laura Keller and four of their children are also buried in the Keller plot in Old Gray.

THOMAS A. KLUTTZ

Thomas Kluttz (1862–1907) is known in Knoxville for his partnership with prolific mail-order architect George F. Barber. The resulting firm, first known as Barber, Kluttz and Graf, produced designs for many houses in Tennessee, North Carolina and other states. Kluttz was born in Rowan County, North Carolina, to Eli and Annie Linn Kluttz, who died young, leaving Thomas and younger sister Mary orphans. They made their home with their mother's brother, a mechanic and house carpenter. Thomas emerged in the 1880s as architect and superintendent for several buildings in that state.[82] The *Raleigh News and Observer* of May 2, 1888, reported that he had completed a "handsome new residence" for Mr. A.E. Rankin that was "perhaps the neatest and most commodious dwelling in East Fayetteville" and identified Kluttz as an "eminent architect" of that city.

Kluttz married Annie Boone in 1888 in Fayetteville, and they had a daughter, Jennie, the following year. In 1891, he completed the Red Springs Hotel in Red Springs, North Carolina. Red Springs was a popular summer mineral springs resort and was known for eighty-five years as the "South's Saratoga." He spent some time working in Georgia, then relocated to Knoxville around 1889. In 1895, Kluttz entered into a business partnership with Barber, working primarily on various Queen Anne and Colonial Revival houses. In 1896, the growing firm moved into the French and Roberts Building, also designed by Barber, a five-story structure on the corner of Depot and Gay Streets. The firm's thirty draftsmen and twenty secretaries occupied an entire floor.

The U.S. Census of 1900 lists the residents of 727 Luttrell Street in Knoxville as architect Thomas A. Klutz [*sic*]; his wife, Annie, a native of Florida; and their daughter, Jennie, age ten. The final Kluttz residence, a two-story Colonial Revival house, was designed and built by Barber and Kluttz in 1903. The house, newly renovated, still stands at 1003 Eleanor Street in what is now known as the Fourth and Gill neighborhood. Several North Carolina houses cited or documented to the firm of Barber and Kluttz

Red Springs Hotel, Thomas Kluttz, architect, Red Springs, Robeson County. *Durwood Barbour Collection of North Carolina Postcards (P077), North Carolina Collection Photographic Archives, Wilson Library, University of North Carolina at Chapel Hill, Chapel Hill, North Carolina.*

also still stand. Over the years, the French and Roberts Building became a series of hotels—Ramsey, Central, Fairway—to accommodate growing rail passenger service. It was condemned and razed for a parking lot in 1963.

In October 1903, Annie Kluttz died following an operation at Knoxville General Hospital. She was only thirty, and Jennie was fourteen. In July 1907, eighteen-year-old Jennie secretly married Harold Newcomer, one of the bookkeepers at M.M. Newcomer & Company. That summer, the architecture firm business was growing and doing designs not just for Knoxville residences. In April, it announced plans for an elaborate hotel, complete with barbershop and Turkish bath, to be built in Bristol, Virginia.[83] In September, the firm submitted bids for a millionaire's $50,000 residence on the Hudson River in New York and a $300,000 courthouse to be erected in Wisconsin.[84] Kluttz died the following November at age forty-five following a brief illness. The *Manufacturers' Record* of December 12 carried an announcement that the firm of Barber and Kluttz, architects, had been discontinued due to Kluttz's death the previous month but that it would continue under Barber's name. Thomas Kluttz is buried in Old Gray alongside his wife, Annie.

CHARLES MCCLUNG

Some of the most beautiful tombstones in Old Gray belong to the McClung family. There are forty-two McClungs here, beginning with patriarch Colonel Charles McClung (1761–1835), who played a significant role in the founding of Knoxville.

McClung was born on his father's farm in Lancaster County, Pennsylvania, in 1761. His parents, Matthew and Martha Cunningham McClung, were of

Scots-Irish descent and came to America around 1740. In 1778, seventeen-year-old Charles, unhappy with the amount of work his father demanded (he claimed this was due to his mechanical aptitude), ran away to Philadelphia, where he gained employment as a clerk. Charles's employer was impressed with his penmanship and recordkeeping ability, and Charles gradually accumulated over $1,000 in savings. He was fired, however, after he was caught flirting with his employer's daughter. After a few years, he returned to the family farm and helped his parents make improvements with the money he had saved.[85]

At some point, McClung acquired rudimentary surveying skills. In 1788, he left the farm again, this time traveling through the valley of Virginia until he reached James White's Fort, now Knoxville, in 1789. White, using his North Carolina land grant, had established his home here in 1786 when the surrounding countryside was still the hunting grounds of the Cherokee and when the Chickamauga-Cherokee Wars were at full tilt (1776–94). In 1790, McClung married White's eldest daughter, Margaret (1771–1827).[86] He was twenty-nine, she was nineteen. His occupation was surveyor. Not much is written about Margaret, but her mother, Mary Lawson White (1742–1819), was lauded in her obituary as someone who "cherished a zealous regard for [her community's] welfare and was ready to make any personal sacrifice to maintain its rights. The stranger ever found her house a home; and multitudes, while this state was still a wilderness, have been refreshed and comforted by her hospitality."[87]

In 1791, William Blount, the governor of the Southwest Territory, moved the territorial capital to White's Fort and renamed it Knoxville in honor of Henry Knox, the American Revolutionary War general and Washington's secretary of war. Soon after, at his father-in-law's request, McClung laid out the original plat of Knoxville. While Knoxville has since expanded to many times its original size, the city's downtown area still roughly follows McClung's 1791 grid. Most of the early street names for the city (e.g., Front Street) were derived from street names in Philadelphia, where McClung had lived for several years. When White, a devout Presbyterian, asked Charles to lay out a town, part of his instructions were "to reserve my

Charles McClung, McClung family plot. *Photo by Judy Loest.*

turnip patch for a church and a burying ground."[88] This parcel became Knoxville's first church, Brick Meeting House, built in 1812, and the turnip patch became the graveyard. The current First Presbyterian Church was built on that site in 1853.

In 1792, McClung surveyed and planned what is now Kingston Pike from Knoxville to Campbell's Station in Farragut. According to the *Index to Indian Affairs* (vol. 1, 1815), he was "appointed commissioner by Gov. Blount to run the boundary line between the United States and the Cherokees as stipulated in the treaty made…on July 2, 1791."

At some point in his peregrinations, McClung also gained legal skills, which propelled him into politics. He was present at the Tennessee constitutional convention in 1796 and was chairman of the committee to draft the state's initial constitution. That year, Knoxville had forty mostly log buildings, public and private, five of which were taverns, and a population of 1,200.

In 1804–5, McClung, along with English-born architect Thomas Hope, designed and built Statesview, the McClung country home on South Peters Road in West Knoxville. It may be that he, like his father-in-law, had grown weary with the city, which had developed into a rowdy frontier capital. White had moved to his farm east of Knoxville in 1800. In 1816, McClung and his eldest surviving son, Matthew, formed Charles McClung and Son, which operated a general store in Knoxville. In 1828, Charles and Matthew helped establish the Knoxville Female Academy and donated land and money for the construction of the academy's school building.

McClung was a member of the board of trustees of Blount College (now the University of Tennessee). He also served as clerk of the Knox County Court (1792–1834). In this position, he served as witness to countless Knox County marriages. In April 1835, just four months before his death, he was elected to the managerial board of the newly organized Agricultural Society for Knox County.

Margaret McClung died in 1827 at age fifty-six and is buried in the First Presbyterian Church Graveyard. Charles McClung died while vacationing at Harrodsburg Springs, Kentucky, on August 9, 1835. He had gone there with his son Matthew to "take the waters" at Graham Springs, a mineral-water spa that flourished in the 1820s and '30s and, by the 1840s, was heralded nationally as the "Saratoga of the West." It was his eighteenth visit. He was seventy-four at the time of his death. Charles was initially buried in Harrodsburg in the private cemetery of Dr. Christopher Graham, owner of the spa. In 1904, McClung's great-grandson Lee McClung had Charles's remains reinterred in the family plot in Old Gray.[89]

Charles and Margaret McClung had ten children. The McClung and White family descendants continued to make contributions to Knoxville's cultural, political and economic development for more than a century. The McClung name is still prominent in Knoxville: McClung Tower, McClung Plaza and the McClung Museum of Natural History and Culture on the UT campus; and the Calvin M. McClung Historical Collection at the East Tennessee History Center. There is also McClung Avenue on Island Home, likely in recognition of the wholesale business partnership of Island Home owner Perez Dickinson and Charles McClung and his two sons.

HELEN ROSS MCNABB

Most people living today in the Knoxville area will recognize the name Helen Ross McNabb (1910–1997) because of the mental health center named in her honor. The impetus behind founding the center came early in her life. In 1914, at the age of four, she visited the "colored" building at East Tennessee State Hospital for the Insane with her nanny, who wanted to visit a friend who worked there. Helen's childhood family home was on a hill about half a mile from the hospital gate, and they walked down the road together. Inside, the images of bars on the windows, locks on the doors and no treatment for the patients made a lasting impression on her young mind and heart. (The hospital was twice renamed—Eastern State Hospital in 1920, then Lakeshore Mental Institute in 1977—and closed in 2012.)

Helen graduated from the University of Tennessee in 1936 with degrees in psychology and sociology. She married Richard "Dick" McTeer McNabb the same year, and they had three children. In 1943, she earned a master's degree in psychology.[90] When Richard left for World War II, Helen returned to UT as an instructor and began taking social case histories for the Home Service Department, established in 1917 to care for veterans and their families.

In 1945, the Child Welfare League of America conducted a survey of children's needs in the Knoxville community. Helen served as chair of the committee to study the possibility of a child guidance clinic and of opening one in Knoxville. Through her work there, she urged the city to establish a child guidance center for the mentally ill. This became the Knoxville Mental

Health Center. The agency quickly grew to also serve adults in 1955. This was the beginning of mental health care in Knoxville.

In 1952, Helen established a volunteer program called Gray Ladies at Eastern State Hospital.[91] The Gray Ladies established a library, helped patients make crafts and started recreation programs such as gardening and book and drama clubs. By 1961, the library had grown to ten thousand volumes and was named the Helen Ross McNabb Library in her honor.

Helen Ross. Knoxville News-Sentinel, *April 3, 1927, 25.*

As first president of the Mental Health Association (1951–54), Helen lobbied for creation of the department of mental health, which had been part of the department of institutions and corrections. Helen continued as a first-line volunteer, giving psychological tests for mental diagnoses and visiting homes of patients who had dropped out of mental health center programs.

In 1962, Helen was awarded the ninth annual Community Services Award of the Council of Community Services. The award is the highest honor in the field of volunteer service to humanitarian, welfare, youth-serving and health agencies. The Knoxville Mental Health Center, of which she was the first chairperson, moved to UT Hospital property in 1968 and was named the Helen Ross McNabb Center. Today, the McNabb Center is the region's leading nonprofit provider of mental health, substance use and social and victim services in East Tennessee, delivering quality care to more than twenty-seven thousand individuals in twenty-five counties.

After a debilitating illness at age sixty-five and until her death in 1997, Helen remained interested in mental health issues and gained much joy and satisfaction at how the center was growing. She reminisced in late life, "That was very important; that I was part of an ongoing movement, that you can make the world a little bit better. We all need to feel needed, don't you think?"

Helen Ross McNabb rests at Old Gray Cemetery with her husband, Dick, and her parents, Lida McClung Ross and William Cary Ross.

This biography was written by Helen's daughter, Eleanor McNabb Kassem, and great-niece Florence "Flossie" McNabb.

FLORENCE DELL MCTEER

Florence Dell McTeer (1889–1971) was the daughter of Ella Hagan McTeer and Richard Perez McTeer. Florence grew up on West Main Avenue in Knoxville with her younger sister Eleanor and three brothers. She attended the University of Tennessee and was a charter member of Chi Omega sorority.

Florence McTeer has the distinction of being the first woman in the United States to hold an administrative position with an agricultural advisory service, being with the University of Tennessee Agricultural Extension service from 1918 until 1955. She supervised and employed the stenographic force for the service and was in charge of all finances. Her office was in Morgan Hall.

In 1914, Miss McTeer was among the "news girls" selling special editions of the *Knoxville News Sentinel* for a YWCA fundraiser. She helped obtain funds for the YWCA Central Building, completed in 1925 and served as volunteer treasurer of the board from 1923 to 1951. Florence made several trips to the YWCA convention in Milwaukee as a delegate representing Knoxville and to the Knoxville Business and Professional Women's Club convention in Cleveland, Ohio.

With her volunteer work for the YWCA and her paid position at the University of Tennessee Extension Service for so many years, a colleague acclaimed Florence as being "one of the most efficient business women I have ever known." In response, Florence said, "Now, who could have said that! I just take tasks as they come."

Florence McTeer also found time to serve on the board of Lawson McGhee Library for thirteen years, was treasurer of the Business Women's Circle of Second Presbyterian Church and a member of the League of Women Voters.

An article in the *Knoxville News Sentinel* in 1928 stated, "Miss Florence McTeer belongs to that class of individuals who are not satisfied with giving less than a full measure of support and enthusiasm to any cause in which they enlist....For years she has been one of the moving spirits of the YWCA. So consistent have been her interest and service here that a friend remarked the other day:

Florence Dell McTeer. *Private collection.*

'To think of the Y.W.C.A. is to think of Florence McTeer.'" From the time of these remarks, her service would extend another twenty-three years.

After her death in 1971, a portrait of Florence McTeer was presented to the YWCA by her great-niece Florence "Flossie" McTeer McNabb. The portrait is hanging there today. Florence McTeer is buried at Old Gray Cemetery along with her parents, her sister Eleanor McTeer McNabb and her three brothers.

This bio was written by Florence "Flossie" McNabb, great-niece of Florence Dell.

EMMA MARTINE MERWIN BECHDOLT

Emma "Decie" Merwin (1894–1961) was a successful artist whom most Knoxvillians today have never heard of. She was born on October 20, 1894, in Middlesboro, Kentucky, to Hubert Merwin of New York and Henrietta "Hettie" Emma Smith of Texas. Hubert earned an engineer of mines degree in 1879 from Columbia College, the oldest undergraduate college of Columbia University in Manhattan. By 1889, Hubert was living in Middlesboro, and there, in 1892, he married Hettie. Around 1905, the family moved to Knoxville, where Hubert became an official with the East Tennessee Iron & Coal Company.

Decie's love of drawing began early. She said that as a child she was never without a pad or notebook so that she could sketch whatever caught her fancy. She graduated from Knoxville High School, possibly in 1910, the year the new high school was completed. She was a member of the Nicholson Art League and the Sketch Club, which met at Knoxville High. She also had private art lessons in Knoxville and credits two teachers, Harriet Wiley with the Art League and Mary Grainger at Knoxville High, as the most influential for her career. At some point, she spent eighteen months studying at the Parsons New School of Design in Boston.[92] In 1917, Decie served as a Red Cross nurse.

In the November 16, 1960 *Knoxville News Sentinel*, she recalled her fondness for the Great Smoky Mountains and the many visits there in her youth long before the area was designated a national park. An excellent horsewoman, Decie rode horseback from Elkmont to Gatlinburg. There was a wagon road, she said, but riding horseback was safer than in a wagon. She hiked Siler's Bald and Mount LeConte before the land was government owned and before the first trails had been created by the Smoky Mountain Hiking Club. And Decie attended Mary Grainger's art camp at Elkmont.

Decie gained national recognition when her illustrations appeared in *Ladies' Home Journal*, and soon she began illustrating children's books. In 1925, she made a bold move in pursuit of a career in art, relocating to New York City. She lived at the Parnassus Club, a boardinghouse for young women on West 115th Street. Room and meals ranged from five to ten dollars a month. Often, two or three women would share a single room. The Parnassus Club was founded and operated by Florence McMillan (a former accompanist to a famous opera diva) in 1921 and was operated by her until 1955. It occupied two buildings: 605 and 612 West 115th Street (directly across the street from each other). Both were originally apartment buildings, constructed in 1903 and 1905, respectively. They are now part of Columbia University.[93]

Decie sailed twice to Europe, once in 1924 with her Knoxville friend Linda Kennedy to England, Scotland and Wales, where they traveled mostly on foot but also by bus and train. The second time she traveled alone (1928–29), spending fifteen months in England and France, much of the time in Brittany and Normandy while completing an illustration assignment for a Clara Laughlin children's travel book, *Where It All Comes True in France* (1929). She said her happiest times were on an island off the coast of Brittany, where she stayed at Château Belle Ile-en-Mer, once owned by Sarah Bernhardt. She loved sitting on the rocky cliffs overlooking the sea and watching the sardine fleet. The ornate château was destroyed during the German occupation of World War II, and the garden is now a golf course. The old

Decie Merwin, 1917. *Blog Books, Mud, and Compost. and Horses Blogspot.*

fort, built in 1859 at Pointe des Poulains, served as Bernhardt's first home and is still there. It is now the Sarah Bernhardt Museum.

In 1930, the U.S. Census shows Decie still living at the Parnassus Club along with 125 other young women. Florence McMillan occupied the penthouse apartment, which had a rooftop garden, which she shared with the boarders. The club was run democratically, with elected officers, practice sessions scheduled for certain hours and rules for gentlemen callers. Although the Parnassus mainly served music students of the Juilliard School of Music and Barnard College, there were also semiprofessional performers and other artists, including writers, and Columbia nursing students, stenographers,

Emma Martine "Decie" Merwin. *Findagrave.com.*

teachers, librarians and salesgirls. Carson McCullers lived there in 1934. Decie had a family member who lived in New York, her father's younger sister Mary Florence Merwin, who lived in Brooklyn for sixty years.[94]

Decie lived nine months of the year in New York and spent her summers and Christmases at her parents' home on Somerset Road in Knoxville. She also contributed to Knoxville art events. Her work was included in the 1928 exhibit of the Fine Arts Society of East Tennessee in Knoxville. Other Knoxville artists included Charles Krutch, Hugh Tyler and Eleanor Wiley. In 1927, she was on the program and publicity committees for the fair at Sterchi Park and designed posters and programs for the night horse shows. Furniture store magnate James G. Sterchi had purchased Chilhowee Park in 1920 and leased it to the East Tennessee Division Fair (the forerunner of the Tennessee Valley Fair). The 1927 fair was a big production, including dog, auto, poultry and livestock shows; exhibits; fireworks; musicals, aerial and roller-skating acts; and more. But the night horse shows were a new event, promising stakes and premiums as high as $10,000, horses from the country's best stables and Madison Square Garden champions.[95] The lake was drained and box seats built for the event, and Decie's posters were put up all over town. Decie also won first prizes in two of the professional fine arts categories.

Decie married John Ernest Bechdolt (1884–1954) in 1934 at the Church of the Ascension in New York City, where they each had lived for several years. Bechdolt was a prolific writer who began as a newspaperman in

Seattle and Kansas City. He is credited, often as Jack Bechdolt, as the author of some six thousand short stories mostly for young readers. Jack's first wife, Mabel Claire Glasier, died in Manhattan in 1933 at the age of forty-three.

Decie illustrated sixty-eight books in her career and collaborated with Jack on a number of children's stories, including the "Dulcie" series. For many years, Jack wrote the books and Decie illustrated. After a few years, she began helping him with the writing. One day, she disagreed with one of his plots, and he said, "If you don't like my plot, why don't you write the book yourself?"[96] She did and then wrote and illustrated seven more books.

Jack died in 1954 at the Southern Pines Sanitarium in Pinebluff, North Carolina, and is buried in Old Gray alongside Decie and her mother and father. Hubert died in 1935, and Hettie died in 1950. Decie died at her brother's home on Riverside Drive in Knoxville on September 7, 1961. She was sixty-six. Several of the children's books she illustrated can be found in the McClung Historical Collection at the East Tennessee History Center and at Lawson-McGhee Public Library.

Laura Richardson

Every year on Memorial Day, volunteers place miniature flags on each Confederate and Union veteran's grave in Old Gray and in the adjacent Knoxville National Cemetery. Knoxville can take pride in the fact that the tradition of placing flags in national cemeteries across America originated with a Knoxville woman, Laura Richardson, who placed the first flags here in May 1874.

Richardson, originally Laura Smith Catlin (1824–1911), a native of Canaan, Connecticut, married Marcus de Lafayette Bearden Sr. (1799–1854) of Knoxville in 1849. Bearden, according to Knoxville historian Jack Neely, was "a wealthy, twice-widowed older man who was involved in riverboating and local industry."[97] Knoxville's Papermill Road is named for the mill he built on Third Creek in the 1830s. Bearden Sr. was also one of the seven men who applied for the charter to establish Gray Cemetery.[98] Laura bore one son, Frank Bearden, before her husband died in 1854.

The widow [next] *married a strong Unionist named David Richardson, and though they went north for safety during part of the Civil War, the*

109

*pair remained in Knoxville after the war was over. She was an admired,
resourceful associate of the women's auxiliary of the Grand Army of the
Republic (GAR), which selected her to chair the committee to decorate the
graves of soldiers at the National Cemetery in late May, 1874.*[99]

According to Laura's letter published in the May 30, 1911 *Knoxville News
Sentinel*, the ladies had always provided roses for the graves, but spring came
so early in 1874 that the rose petals fell to the ground as soon as the bushes
were touched.

*Passing the large plate window of Cowan, McClung & Co., I stopped,
for in that window were great rolls of small flags. Hurrying to the office
of Maj. Prosser, (Chairman of the Men's committee), I said, if your
committee will buy these flags, my committee will get them ready. As an
equal partner to Burrow & Terry [Burr & Terry, Knoxville lumber
dealers], I wrote to them to furnish me 3,000 wood sticks two feet
long, sharpened at one end, and send them to the homes of the committee
women. We had not quite two days to get the flags ready. The members of
the men's committee must have cut the flags out as they came to us ready to
be put on the sticks. How we did work for nearly two days, hardly taking
time for our meals, but at 12 o'clock the night before Decoration Day, the
caretaker of the national cemetery sent word to us that "every grave was
bearing its flag." As the ladies' carriage followed that of the speakers,
I remember seeing ex-President Andrew Johnson standing up with hat
in hand bowing this way and that to those who had gathered along the
thoroughfare. So, by this, the first time he was ever present, Decoration
Day established itself, May 30, 1874....As we entered the cemetery,
every flag was gently waving mutely, saying: "For this we gave our lives."
It is beginning to be known now that Knoxville was the first city to use
flags to decorate the graves of the soldiers in the national cemetery, since
which time the United States has now sanctioned it and now furnishes
suitable flags.*

In 1903, Laura returned to her birthplace in Canaan, Connecticut,
spending her summers there and her winters in New Marlborough,
Massachusetts.[100] Laura died in Canaan on February 3, 1911, at age eighty-
six. Her obituary, published in the February 10 *Boston Globe* and *Boston Evening
Transcript*, included the story of her creation of a national tradition:

Originated a National Custom: Mrs. Laura S. Richardson First Suggested Placing Small Flags on the Graves of Civil War Soldiers
It was in Knoxville, in 1874, that Mrs. Richardson originated the present custom of decorating the graves of the soldier dead in national cemeteries. She was chairman of a committee of four women to procure flowers for decorating 3,033 graves in the National Cemetery there. While walking along the streets she saw great piles of miniature flags in a store window. Like a flash the idea came to her that they would be fit emblems to deck the graves of the nation's fallen heroes. The flags were provided with sticks from the mill, and, for the first time in the nation's history, the red, white, and blue was used on May 30, 1874, in the decoration of soldiers' graves….Mrs. Richardson's maiden name was Laura Smith Catlin. Her maternal grandfather, Captain Ebenezer Smith, was a captain in the army of General Washington; hence, she was entitled to the honor of being "a Real Daughter" of the Revolution. She passed her summers in New Marlborough and her winters in Canaan, CT. She is survived by one son, Frank C. Bearden of Knoxville.

Laura's husbands and her son Frank are buried in Old Gray. Laura is buried in New Marlborough Cemetery in New Marlborough, Berkshire County, Massachusetts, along with her parents and seven siblings.

WILLIAM CARY ROSS

William Cary Ross (1879–1956), the third and last child of Martin Luther Ross and Helen Nellie Cary Ross, was born in Knoxville not long after his family moved from Anderson County, Tennessee. Martin Ross started a candy manufacturing and wholesale grocery business that operated at various times and locations in downtown Knoxville, often in partnership. They were gutted by fire twice and ended up operating as M.L. Ross & Company on Gay Street. Ross was fond of saying that he began his career sweeping floors and filling orders in his father's grocery.

The business did so well that Martin was able to send his son to the new Baker-Himel School on the southeast corner of Highland Avenue and Twelfth Street. The school was established in 1889 by Lewis Baker and Charles M. Himel of the University of Virginia. They had been recruited by several prominent Knoxville citizens. The object of the school (also called the University School) was to prepare boys for college. Students completing the academic course were admitted without further examination to the University of Tennessee, the University of Virginia, Harvard or Yale. The school's reputation became so extensive that it attracted students from as far north and east as Illinois and Connecticut and as far south as Louisiana and Texas. Attendance averaged about one hundred; about a dozen students were boarders. The school operated until 1913. Cecil Baker, son of Lewis Baker, would later marry Ross's sister Mary.

In 1893 or 1894, Martin Ross built a handsome three-story house at 1415 Laurel Avenue in White's Addition, named for Hugh Lawson White, who had a house there. Ross and attorney George Pickle were among the first to build mansions there. Just thirty years before, the hillside was a barren, bloody battlefield surrounding the Union-held Fort Sanders, which withstood the two-week Siege of Knoxville in November 1863. By 1900, the tree-lined, exclusive neighborhood, high on a green hillside removed from the industrial pollution of downtown Knoxville, was attracting Knoxville's leading industrialists, including Max Arnstein, Matthew McClung and Pat Roddy. It was also home to early university professors and administrators. The neighborhood is now called Fort Sanders, and the Martin Ross house, retaining its original exterior, was converted to apartments in the 1930s. It operates today as Laurel Terrace Apartments, a popular residence for University of Tennessee students.

Martin Ross died suddenly in 1899 at age forty-nine while William Ross was in his first year at Yale. The death notice in the June 30, 1899 *Bolivar (TN) Bulletin* stated, "Hon. M.L. Ross of Knoxville, Vice President of the Mechanics' National Bank and President of the Chamber of Commerce, dropped dead at the breakfast table one morning last week of apoplexy." Apoplexy results from a cerebral hemorrhage or stroke. William Ross graduated from Yale in 1900 with a BS degree in philosophy and was immediately elected president of M.L. Ross & Company.

Ross reminisced over the years of those early days in Knoxville, recalling mule-drawn streetcars and how he began courting after joining the Cotillion Club, often double-dating, since he and a friend could hire a closed carriage with coachman for four dollars a night. At a wedding reception in 1901, he met Eliza "Lida" Mills McClung (1882–1968), who, he later wrote, seemed to him "the sweetest, most gracious and charming person I had ever seen; and, after all these years, I have never changed my mind." The couple married the following year. For one summer they lived on a farm near Boyd's Bridge, then they built a home at 1515 West Clinch Avenue, where their two daughters, Lawson (Lawson McClung Sullivan) and Helen (Helen Ross

McNabb) were born. The area is now part of the UT campus and contains a cluster of upscale apartment complexes.

In 1905, M.L. Ross & Company merged with H.T. Hackney. William Ross, who was good friends with Hackney president Ben Morton, became chairman of the board. Ross, Morton and Hugh Sanford became a successful business triumvirate despite Knoxville's growing stagnation. They called themselves "The Three Musketeers" or "The 100 Percent Club" and, by 1923, were Knoxville's premier financiers. Over the next twenty years, Ross, Morton and Sanford went into mining, manufacturing, wholesaling, retailing, real estate, lumber and contracting enterprises, one of which was the Farragut Hotel, built in 1917.

In 1907, Ross organized Cherokee Country Club, buying the land, building the clubhouse and becoming its first president (1907–10). In 1909, he was elected vice-president and treasurer of the Knoxville Woolen Mill. While the mill was the largest of its kind in the South, there was no longer a demand for the company's type of cloth, and the outdated machinery was not able to produce a salable substitute. Ross tried for three years to adapt the machinery to meet the demand for new woolen products but was not successful. He decided to liquidate the assets of the company, showing a sense of timing that served him well in other business ventures. The stockholders were satisfied, but the laying off of mill employees had a negative economic impact on the city. In September 1918, Ross volunteered for World War I but was rejected by the U.S. Air Corps due to poor vision.

In 1911, the Rosses decided they wanted to live in "the country" and purchased land along the Tennessee River in the area known as Lyons Bend. By this time, according to historian Bruce Wheeler, urban neighborhoods had fallen into ruin and the downtown area had deteriorated. Wealthier citizens fled to new suburbs on the city's periphery, such as North Hills and Sequoyah Hills. By 1913, a streetcar traveled all the way to Lyons View Pike, paving the way for residential development in the area. The William Cary Ross home on Lyons View Pike, known as Rostrevor, was designed by Barber & McMurry and constructed in 1921. The home was a hub of social events—teas, luncheons, musicales, dinner dances, buffets and garden suppers. It hosted influential guests such as Clarence Darrow following the Scopes trial in 1925.

The Rostrevor garden, designed by Ross and managed by Lida, was one of the first in Knoxville to be inspired during the formal garden revival movement of the early twentieth century. The Italian garden, with its superb view of the Tennessee River and the Smoky Mountains beyond, was widely acclaimed and a popular destination for garden club pilgrimages. It was included in several gardening books, including *Beautiful Gardens in America* (1924), *A History of Homes and Gardens in Tennessee* (1931) and *The Golden Age of American Gardens: Proud Owners, Private Gardens* (1991). When the Lookout Mountain Garden Club came to Knoxville to evaluate the city's qualifications for membership in the National Garden Clubs in 1926, the lawn party and tea at Rostrevor, complete with the Craig Whittle Springs Orchestra on the veranda, likely sealed membership approval. Although Rostrevor was demolished in 1969 and much of Ross's old grounds, including the wildflower garden, were flattened for Cherokee Country Club's tennis courts and other projects, Rostrevor garden is still intact in the backyard at the home of Ross's grandson William Ross "Sandy" McNabb.

In his retirement, Ross turned to his lifelong love of carpentry and began carving small wood sculptures—birds, flowers, people—that he gave to friends. He also published two books, *A Scrapbook for My Grandchildren* (1941) and *It's Up to You: A Way to a Better Life* (1950), both of which stressed personal development, self-reliance and hard work. His strong work ethic was reflected in his last will and testament, which included a stipulation that his five grandchildren would inherit "if they make decent, useful citizens of themselves" and do not "turn out to be indolent, improvident, wild or worthless, time-wasting idlers."

MARY UTOPIA ROTHROCK

Libraries and librarians have always represented some resistance to political moments. Public book warehouses have been championed as the most democratic places in America, certainly the most welcoming and helpful to immigrants. Now seems an especially pertinent time to write about a librarian whose remarkable achievements changed not only her city's but also the region's history. Knoxville, Tennessee, was lucky to have had this unique library pioneer—a woman with the intelligence, ambition and audacity to challenge conventional wisdom—but, like most unsung heroes in the library profession, she is largely unknown, even in Knoxville, except by historians, academics and library lovers. The Friends of the Knox County Public Library set out to change that. In 2010, the Friends opened the Rothrock Used Book Shop in Lawson McGhee Library downtown. On Wednesday, September 19, 2018, her

Mary Utopia Rothrock.
McClung Historical Collection, Knox County Public Library.

birthday was celebrated in Old Gray and officially named Mary Utopia Rothrock Day.

Mary Utopia Rothrock (1890–1976), or Topie, as she was affectionately called by friends and family, was many things besides a librarian, most prominently, community activist, historian, author and editor. She wrote two textbooks, *Discovering Tennessee* (nine editions published between 1936 and 1961) and *This Is Tennessee: A School History* (four editions published between 1963 and 1973). She edited the first major comprehensive history of Knox County and Knoxville, *The French Broad-Holston County: A History of Knox County, Tennessee* (eight editions published between 1946 and 1972). She also published and edited numerous articles and wrote *Fifty Years of Lawson-McGhee Library, 1917–1967*. All told, Rothrock has twenty-two works in forty-seven publications and 561 library holdings. She accomplished a great deal more.

Many who knew Rothrock would say that she was also a feminist long before the word was familiar. She was definitely subversive in reshaping the Tennessee library system. Spoken of locally as a "red-haired dynamo," she was also devoted to fighting for women's rights. During the suffragist movement, one Knoxvillian said of Rothrock that she is "a dangerous woman—you never know where she is gonna bust out next." In 1930, she successfully debated Knoxville mayor James Trent, who, as an answer to high unemployment, wanted women to give up their jobs to men. He had nothing further to say following her reply:

> *You assume that your jobless men could take the place of your employed woman. But could they. Society would be injured more by the maladjustment set up by men in women's jobs, than it is by unemployed men. Women get their jobs and hold their jobs because they can do the work better than men....When you deprive women of the possibility of economic independence, you have enslaved them.*[101]

How did such a maverick come to be? One can start with her Wikipedia biography.

Born in Brick Church in Giles County, Tennessee, Rothrock grew up in Trenton, Tennessee. She was the youngest of five children of John Rothrock, a Presbyterian minister, and his wife, Utopia (Herron) Rothrock. She attended public schools in Milan, Tennessee, and Somerville, Tennessee, and the Ward Seminary in Nashville. She graduated from Vanderbilt University in 1912 with a master of science degree, and the New York School of Library Science in Albany in 1914 with a BLS degree. While in New York, she worked as an assistant at the New York State Library. Rothrock returned to Tennessee in 1915 to serve as Head of Circulation at the Cossitt Library in Memphis.

Brick Church, according to the 1895 census, was little more than a hamlet with a population of twenty-five. There was a post office but no railroad service. Trenton had a population of about two thousand in 1900. The Rothrocks were members of the South's new middle class but certainly were not wealthy. During that same period, a Presbyterian minister in Nashville, a much larger city, had a salary of only $600 a year. Mary, the youngest of five children, probably wore hand-me-downs, and the family likely depended on meals from parishioners. Topie's mother, Utopia, died three months after Topie's birth. When Topie was six, her father married her mother's cousin Tennessee "Tennie" Byrn, who became, affectionately, "Fannie" to Topie and her four older siblings.

During her studies at Vanderbilt, Rothrock visited the Cossitt Library in Memphis. Before this visit, she had wanted to be a writer, but after experiencing the impressive Romanesque Cossitt, she knew instantly that she wanted to be a librarian. And she knew where she wanted to study: the New York State Library School in Albany. Getting accepted there was not easy; entrance requirements and competition were tough. That Rothrock chose Albany over Atlanta says much about her courage, not only because she chose the premier library school at that time, but also that she was a young woman with modest financial means going alone from a small southern town to a large northern city like Albany.

Nevertheless, after earning her master's degree from Vanderbilt in 1913, Rothrock, with the loan from a cousin, boarded a train, possibly at the newly opened Beaux-Arts Union Station, and headed north. Mary Mallory, in her essay for the *Library Quarterly*, elaborated: "Most of the female collegians of Rothrock's generation came from middle-class families; however, at that time southern universities, public or private, admitted few women. Her graduation from Vanderbilt University (BS, 1911; MS, 1912) was therefore exceptional, her choice of institution for library training even more so. Rothrock attended the New York State Library School in Albany for two years and received her professional degree in librarianship in 1914. Only a few of her southern peers chose programs other than the Library School at the Carnegie Library of Atlanta."[102]

Rothrock's time in New York proved to be transformative. In an epilogue to *Fresh Eyes: The Freshman English Essays of Mary Utopia Rothrock* (1907), her great-niece Laura Herron Meacham Keane says that after earning her master's degree from Vanderbilt in 1913, Rothrock chose to attend the school in Albany. Keane writes:

> *There were 70 students enrolled in the program, coming from 22 states, from Vermont to California; Topie was the lone southerner. There were eight students from Norway and Denmark, whom Topie describes as "keen-witted, observant, and outgoing."*
>
> *Topie earned her expenses by writing reviews of books being considered for inclusion in the buying guide for small libraries in the New York state library system* [her title was assistant in the acquisitions section].... *Topie thrived, saying "these were truly pioneer days in professional librarianship... the double load of school and job was time-consuming, but I do not recall that it was burdensome. In fact, the personal friendships and the intellectual stimulus of these two years were long-lasting...The Albany years opened up a new world to me. They were challenging and satisfying in many ways. Albany was nearly a thousand miles in distance from Somerville* [TN] *but more than a thousand in its occupations, ways of life."*

Rothrock, during her tenure as library director, was considered by fellow members in the Southeastern Library Association (SELA) "snobbish about the library school training of her employees, and several times backed out of employment negotiations...for Atlanta graduates." "If we can't have both thorough training and native ability," Rothrock wrote, "we prefer the latter. Of course we would like also a good disposition and adaptability. In short we want Albany quality."

In 1915, Rothrock returned to work at the Cossitt as head of circulation. It was at the Cossitt Library in 1916 that Knoxville businessman and philanthropist Colonel Charles McClung McGhee discovered her. McGhee's beloved twenty-three-year-old daughter, May Lawson McGhee, died in childbirth in 1883. The infant died a couple of weeks later. McGhee began planning a new library in memory of May and began a search for a chief librarian. He was soon "impressed by that little red-haired librarian in Memphis." McGhee persuaded Rothrock to come to Knoxville. His only advice, "Try to look older."

Rothrock, only twenty-six, helped plan, stock, staff and organize the new Knoxville library (then at the corner of Market and Commerce Streets) and oversaw the establishment of the citywide branch system. Knoxville historian Jack Neely, at the Old Gray celebration for Rothrock, wondered what her favorite books may have been. A partial list from her midlife can be found in the April 13, 1941 *Knoxville News Sentinel*. The book page editor had solicited selected readers' lists of six books they would take to an ivory tower retreat. Rothrock's was among the forty-two entries published. Typical for the time and place, the title garnering the most votes was *Psalms*. Rothrock's list, in this order, was *Montaigne's Essays*, *The Oxford Book of English Verse*, *The Story of Mankind* by Hendrik Van Loon, *The Forsyte Saga*, *Leaves of Grass* and *Dawn of Tennessee Valley and Tennessee History*.

The interesting selection is Van Loon's, which was popular at that time but also controversial. Although the target audience was children, the book was recommended to and popular with adults. Van Loon was awarded the first Newberry Medal in 1921 and, in 1942, was named among "America's 93 greatest living authors," a list compiled by a public ballot. But like H.G. Wells's *The Outline of History*, the book also faced popular resistance. Several libraries banned it from their collections. Like Wells, Van Loon had included in *The Story of Mankind* the newest astronomical, geological and biological findings, marking him a Darwinian theorist. Creationist Christians, offended by the extended treatment of evolution at the beginning of the book and no mention of creation or miraculous works, were successful in banning the book from some classrooms and libraries, thus hampering its national distribution.

Van Loon was born in Rotterdam, Holland, but immigrated to the United States in 1902 and lectured on European history from 1915 to 1916. It's entirely possible that Rothrock, who graduated from the Albany library school in 1915, attended one of his lectures. She surely would have known of him. That his book was third on her list to take to a retreat tells us what an indelible impression it made on her. Near the end of Van Loon's book, he, too, mentions the influence of Rothrock's first book choice: "I was born and educated in an atmosphere of the old-fashioned liberalism which had followed the discoveries of Darwin and the other pioneers of the nineteenth century. As a child, I happened to spend most of my waking hours with an uncle who was a great collector of the books written by Montaigne, the great French essayist of the sixteenth century."[103]

Rothrock became Tennessee Librarian Association (TLA) president in 1920 and was elected a second time in 1928. She organized and founded the Southeastern Library Association (SELA) in Chattanooga in 1920 and became its first president. Rothrock was the first recipient of the ALA Lippencott Award for distinguished service to the library profession (1938); was ALA president (1946–47); and was awarded Honorary Life Membership of the Tennessee Library Association (1956). She also cofounded the East Tennessee Historical Society and persuaded Calvin McClung to donate his personal collection to the library, thus creating the McClung Collection, which became the core of the organization. In 1941, she was a member of the joint ALA, Red Cross and USO committee that supervised a nationwide drive to provide books to the U.S. armed forces.

Her name was in the local newspaper almost weekly during the 1920s and '30s for her library work and activism, both in writing and many public speaking engagements. From 1934 to 1949, she served as TVA's supervisor of libraries and brought the first bookmobiles to people in remote areas.[104]

Rothrock wrote and edited many articles about Tennessee and wrote two high-school textbooks on the state's history. In 1948, she was awarded an Honorary Doctor of Letters from the University of Chattanooga. From 1948 to 1955, she was a Knox County librarian.

One of her colleagues wrote, "'Topie' knows all the answers and is one of the smartest persons in the library profession." Her modest grave marker in Old Gray belies her great influence on the Knox County Public Library system and, through it, the people of East Tennessee.

WILLIAM RULE

One of the most prominent people in Old Gray is William Rule (1839–1928), beloved two-term mayor of Knoxville and the editor of, first, the *Knoxville Daily Chronicle* and, later, the *Knoxville Journal*. He is best known for mentoring the young Adolph Ochs, who started working for Rule at age eleven and famously bought the *New York Times* in 1896 at age thirty-eight. Because the sixty-year relationship between these two men was influential in shaping the greatest, most powerful newspaper in the free world, it is difficult to examine the life of one without considering the other.

An easy assumption today is that the people buried in Old Gray in the early twentieth century came from privileged backgrounds, but for the majority, that is far from the truth. The next generation of Knoxville men and women may have moved into a higher socioeconomic status, but most of their parents worked hard to rise out of poverty. William Rule and Adolph Ochs are examples of the norm. Both men were descendants of German immigrants, Rule's great-grandfather having come from Hessen-Darmstadt to Virginia in the late 1700s, and Ochs's father coming from Fürth, Bavaria, to Kentucky in 1848. Both men were largely self-educated, and they both inherited their mothers' love of reading and their fathers' gentleness and profound respect for fairness and human individuality.

Portrait of William Rule. *History of Mayors, City of Knoxville, Mayor's Office.*

William Rule, the eldest of seven children, was born in a log cabin (the same in which his father, Frederick, was born) in Stock Creek, about seven miles south of downtown Knoxville. At age nineteen, he married Lucy Maxey and made an unsuccessful attempt to run a hardware store on Gay Street. At age twenty-one, he went to work on William Brownlow's newspaper the *Knoxville Whig*. There, he did everything from writing news and setting type to mailing and delivering papers. When the paper folded at the onset of the Civil War two years later, Rule enlisted in the Union army infantry. He was quickly promoted to lieutenant, then to adjutant. Throughout the war, he carried the Bible, a book of Shakespeare's plays and a collection of Robert Burns's poems. One of the few quotes from Rule was a humorous remark about a friend, a Confederate soldier who, after the war, asked if he (Rule) had ever shot at him. Rule told him, "I did not, for you were in the cavalry and I couldn't catch you."

For a time after the war, Rule was a correspondent for papers in Nashville, Memphis, New York and Cincinnati, and then he was employed as city editor for three more years on the reinstated *Whig*. For brief periods, he was county court clerk and postmaster. In 1870, he founded the *Knoxville Daily Chronicle* and in 1885 the *Knoxville Journal*. He was elected Knoxville mayor twice (1873 and 1898).

Adolph Ochs was born in 1858 in Cincinnati, the eldest of six children. In 1864, the family moved to Knoxville in search of opportunity. Julius Ochs held various civic positions—alderman, tax assessor, justice of the peace, part-time rabbi—but was not a good businessman. Adolph knew early on that he would have to augment the family income. He began his first job as a carrier at the *Chronicle* in 1869 at age eleven. Like the young Rule before him, Ochs accepted any task no matter how menial. Over the course of eight years, he moved from sweeping offices and delivering papers into progressively more responsible jobs. He called his years at the newspaper his "high school and university."

Rule earned many distinctions in his long career. He was a charter member of the Lawson-McGhee Library and secretary of the board for twelve years, a charter member of the board of governors for Knoxville General Hospital, a member of the Republican National Committee (1876–84) and a delegate to the Republican National Convention (1876). As mayor, he established the city waterworks and a smallpox hospital. Though not an alumnus of the University of Tennessee, he served fifty years on the board of trustees and was secretary for several years prior to his resignation in 1918. Passing the campus one day, he looked at the trees on the slope of "The Hill" and remarked, "There is one of the few things that reminds me of my age. I was one of the Trustees who authorized that many of those trees should be set out." The university bestowed on him an honorary master's degree in 1918.

Rule spoke out against Appalachian stereotypes (which were beginning to take shape after the Civil War), arguing that people from the region had normal levels of intelligence but suffered due to southern states' lack of funding for schools. In 1873, wealthy Memphis financier Moses Wicks, angered over a column by Rule that criticized Wicks's mismanagement of his railroad and banking enterprises, challenged Rule to a duel. Rule refused, saying, "I recognize no heathenish, so-called code of honor....You might take my life or I might take yours and yet not a single feature of the publication complained of would be changed by the results." The story was published in the *New York Times* and subsequently lauded in newspaper editorials across the country. After this incident, public sentiment caused the end of dueling as a means of resolving disputes.

In 1896, Ochs, taking control of the *New York Times*, mortgaged and risked everything to "conduct a high standard newspaper, clean, dignified and trustworthy." The *Times* won the first Pulitzer Prize for journalism in 1918. Ochs received honorary degrees from six universities and came to be known as the "Titan of Humanity" for his lifelong philanthropy. Probably the most famous of his charitable initiatives is the Hundred Neediest Cases Fund, a campaign established by the *Times* in 1912 and that continues today. The fund's history is an interesting story in itself, a Christmas story that makes Adolph Ochs the George Bailey of his time. In its 105 years, the fund has raised $288 million for those struggling in New York. The 2016–17 campaign, which ran from November 13 to February 10, raised $6,177,625—more than $500,000 above the previous year's total. For the first time, it extended its reach globally when the International Rescue Mission, a worldwide aid group based in New York that helps refugees and vulnerable populations, joined the campaign.

Biographers of Adolph Ochs argue that the *Times*'s commitment to objectivity may have originated in Ochs's personal, almost reverent, admiration for William Rule. Like Rule, Ochs viewed his newspaper as a trust, upholding the principals on which the First Amendment is based. He established a code of ethics for the *New York Times* that he published as an oath in his first issue: "To give the news impartially, without fear or favor, regardless of party, sect or interests involved."

For a few years in the mid- to late 1870s, the *Chronicle* was owned by William "Parson" Brownlow, and Ochs had the opportunity to witness both Brownlow's and editor Rule's strongly differing views about the place of opinion in a newspaper. Writing in the March 7, 1879 *Chattanooga Times*, Ochs stated that his association with the two men influenced him greatly. He called Brownlow "a harsh man; a reliable hater; not particular to be politically consistent, eager to carry any point he set his head or heart on; endowed with a violent temper and a vindictive nature....We confess no admiration, personal or other, for the dead Governor and Senator. His political methods were especially distasteful....He was always, to our mind, the same violent, and if trusted with power, dangerous man." As owner of the *Times*, Ochs chose to practice an objectivity that reflected the views of his "guide, philosopher, and friend," William Rule.

In 1884, Ochs married Effie Wise, the daughter of Rabbi Isaac Mayer Wise of Cincinnati, the leading exponent of Reform Judaism in America and the founder of Hebrew Union College. In 1928, Ochs built the Mizpah Congregation Temple in Chattanooga in memory of his parents, Julius and Bertha Ochs. When Adolph died in 1858, the best and most capable person to take over the *Times* was his only surviving child, daughter Iphigene Ochs Sulzberger, but such an appointment was impossible in a patriarchal world—women were still unable to vote. Her husband, Arthur Sulzberger, became publisher, and her son, Ochs's great-grandson Arthur Ochs Sulzberger Jr., has been publisher of the *New York Times* since 1992. One of the longest and most interesting obituaries in the *Times* is that of Iphigene "Iffey" Ochs Sulzberger, February 27, 1990.

By his last decade, Rule was so beloved by his community that civic organizations hosted annual luncheons in his honor. He was esteemed and respected by journalists throughout the country and, at age eighty-nine, honored nationally after *Time* magazine called him "the oldest active editor in the U.S." Just weeks before his death, he was still arriving at the office every morning at 8:00 a.m. and leaving at 5:30 p.m. Ochs attended Rule's eighty-second and eighty-ninth birthday celebrations. At the latter, Ochs, reading from a letter he had written for the occasion, said, "Captain Rule was a hero to me when I was a lad 10 years of age, and in the 60 years that have elapsed since then, he has not only maintained that eminence in my mind, but has steadily risen higher in my esteem."

Just two and a half months later, on July 26, 1928, William Rule died in Fort Sanders Hospital following surgery for a ruptured appendix. Ochs was unable to attend the funeral but sent a telegram, and the July 28 issue of the *New York Times* included a memorial headed "Tribute by Knoxville to Captain Rule; People of All Walks of Life at Funeral of Dean of American Editors." The following year, Ochs returned to Knoxville to attend a posthumous celebration of Rule's ninetieth birthday. During that visit, he asked Henry Collins, the man who taught him how to set type fifty years earlier at the *Chronicle*, to accompany him to Rule's grave in Old Gray, where he placed a large wreath.

Ochs died suddenly on April 9, 1935, at age seventy-seven while visiting Chattanooga. Even after nearly forty years of living in New York City, he always called Chattanooga "home." For decades he planned to be buried there, but in 1933, he purchased a grave site in Temple Israel Cemetery at Mount Hope in Westchester County, New York. He chose Temple Israel primarily because it would be easier for his beloved daughter Iphigene to visit. Also, Iphigene's husband's family, the Sulzbergers, were interred in Temple Israel.

Archived in the New York Public Library, among 137 boxes of the Adolph S. Ochs papers, is the four-decade correspondence between Rule and Ochs. Also included is a scrapbook Ochs assembled during the year following Rule's death. In it are obituaries and clippings about the career of "Captain William Rule, Knoxville, Tennessee."

The *New York Times* has been awarded 122 Pulitzer Prizes (3 in 2017)—more than any other news organization—and, in these troubling times, continues to uphold Ochs's promise to give the American people "the whole story, without fear or favor." As William Rule's 178th birthday approaches, Old Gray pays tribute to the man who devoted over sixty years of highly principled editorial service to Knoxville, a contribution that continues to influence journalistic integrity worldwide today.

William Rule and Adolph Ochs were among the first ten journalists inducted into the Tennessee Newspaper Hall of Fame in 1969.

HERMAN SCHUBERT

Herman Alexander Schubert (1843–1885) was the celebrity chef of his day. A native of Gnessen, a province of Posen, Prussia, and the eldest of six children, Herman arrived in New York in 1857 and remained there three years. About 1860, he came to Nashville, where he worked in the restaurant and retail liquor business until 1865. For the next two years, he continued in the same business in Chattanooga and in Grainger and Union Counties.

In 1868, he married the older widow Hannah Beeler Turner (1833–1886) of Union County. Hannah had one child, a daughter, age fifteen. Hannah's first husband, Jacob Turner, died of smallpox in 1862, the year Union County ridges and valleys became the main route of troop movement for both Confederate and Union soldiers and a route for deserters, fleeing enslaved persons and Unionists seeking asylum behind Union lines.

In 1872, Herman and Hannah had a son, Nicholas Alexander, and in 1874, the family moved to Knoxville, where Herman found employment running the restaurant in Nick Eifler's St. Nicholas Hotel on West Cumberland Street. The restaurant, likely the only public dining room in town at the time, quickly became a popular dinner and event venue. Notices of house specialties like green sea turtle soup and oysters appeared almost daily in the *Knoxville Chronicle*. According to the *Chronicle*'s description of a banquet attended by members of the Knoxville Bar, "oysters were served in every style, prepared in the highest style of the art, as Schubert knows so well how to do." Herman, by then known as General Schubert, also had the best bar in town and advertised himself as the sole agent for Kauffman's lager beer, a major Cincinnati brand that sold fifty thousand barrels a year in its flourishing southern trade.

After five or six years, Herman bought Eifler out and began adding to his already large building. On October 6, 1881, the *Chronicle* reported that "Mr. H. Schubert, popular restaurateur, opened his 'European Hotel' on Cumberland Street, west of Gay, yesterday and put his porters out… prepared to entertain guests for lodging in princely style." The hotel had about one hundred rooms and was one of the first buildings to have electric lights, thanks to the Schuyler Electric Light Company, which had set up a generator plant, fueled by an iron boiler, on Gay Street near Cumberland. Hotel amenities also included private bathrooms, billiard and bar rooms, a telegraph and transfer office and even a barbershop. The gentlemen's parlor was especially popular with businessmen and politicians traveling by rail. The "Divine" Sarah Bernhardt ate there when in town for a performance at the Staub Theatre.

Goodspeed Publishing Company's 1887 *History of Tennessee* includes Schubert's Hotel among Knoxville's first-class hotels, along with Hattie House, Atkin House and Lamar House. The Schuberts, by then joined by Herman's brother Jacob and sister Rosalie, lived in the hotel. The 1880 U.S. Census shows Rosalie as "keeping house" and Jacob as a bartender. Herman and Nicholas continued to live there after Hannah's death in 1886. In 1887, Herman's other three siblings were still living, one in Chicago, one in Australia and one in Berlin.

Well into the 1940s, local newspapers fondly remembered Schubert's Hotel as "the swankiest spot in town" and proprietor Schubert as a model host, "a jovial, pleasant, *bon vivant* fellow with a wide reputation for hospitality." One article included a description of an old Christmas dinner menu found among the personal effects of Frank McClung. Alongside the raw oysters, mock turtle soup and a variety of entrées with French sauces—mutton, venison, beef, turkey, red snapper and salmon—were also mallard ducks, young pig and opossum.

In 1882, Herman was appointed commissary general to Tennessee governor Robert Love Taylor. Herman served two years in that position but continued to cater Governor Taylor's events. An example was the Nashville–Atlanta leg of President and Mrs. Grover Cleveland's twenty-three-day Goodwill Tour by rail of the Midwest and South. An article in the October 27, 1887 *Pulaski (TN) Citizen* states that the governor's train, carrying Taylor, other Nashville dignitaries and press in a private car, preceded the president's train by fifteen minutes. The trains were met by "crowds and pandemonium as they passed through each small town." The editor added: "Gen. Herman Schubert of the governor's staff is a princely caterer. He provisioned a state room of the governor's car with the choicest consumables which he served with princely liberality."

Herman experienced tragedy in his final decade. In 1885, his brother Jacob, age forty, committed suicide. The death certificate listed the cause of death as opium poison (morphine). On Thursday, August 22, 1889,

Herman was with a group of Knoxville businessmen making an excursion on the new railroad from Knoxville to Cumberland Gap. At Flat Creek, just twenty-two miles northeast of Knoxville, the rear car broke loose and tumbled twenty-three feet down an embankment, leaving four men dead and twenty-seven injured. The afternoon paper proclaimed, "The Flower of Our Citizenry in an Awful Railroad Wreck!" Herman survived but with both legs broken. Other survivors included A.J. Albers, Peter Kern and W.W. Woodruff. Doctors worked until midnight dressing wounds and setting broken limbs. Knoxville businesses closed, and thousands gathered in the streets that night. It was the worst disaster in the city since the Civil War.

A *Knoxville News Sentinel* article on March 8, 1945, filled in some of the intervening history of the Schubert Hotel. The article covered the fire that destroyed the Cumberland Hotel the night before. The Cumberland was the last incarnation of the Schubert building. After Herman's death, the hotel went into slow decline, first becoming the Flanders, then the Appalachian and, finally, the Cumberland. Recalling Schubert's Hotel as the building's "colorful period," the article reads:

> *The old hotel was famous in those days for its cuisine and headquarters of prominent politicians. Notable among the latter was Gov. Bob Taylor who considered Schubert's a second home....Schubert's dining room was in the nature of an institution in Knoxville in those days....Oysters were not so easy to come by then as now, and* [after dances at the Cotillion Room a couple of doors down] *the swains of the city would bring their belles to Schubert's for oysters and other seafoods. The dining room was quite large and situated on the first floor fronting Gay Street...* [and] *tastefully decorated with paintings by local artists Lloyd Branson, Adelia Lutz Armstrong, and Henry Curtis.*

The hotel occupied the corner of Gay and Cumberland across from the Bijou Theatre, which is now a parking lot.

Herman's obituary states that he never entirely recovered from his injuries and that financial difficulties followed. He died suddenly and seemingly painlessly in his bed early one morning. His funeral was held in his home, which was then at 114 West Main Street. His obituary lauds his bootstrap success as a hotelier, his hospitality and his acts of generosity. Chief among the latter were his Christmas ("and oftener") dinners for the inmates of the St. John's orphanage and Margaret McClung Girls' Industrial Home. "The news of his death," it states, "will be read with sincere regret by thousands of people."[105]

Hannah Schubert died in 1886 and is also buried in Old Gray, along with Nicholas and his wife, Cora.

TOLMIE FAMILY

The Tolmie father and son buried in Old Gray were second- and third-generation railroad men, descendants of Scottish immigrant Alexander McDonald Tolmie (1822–1902), an engineer and machinist who came to America in 1848 and settled in Nashville. Alexander was hired by the Nashville & Chattanooga Railroad while it was being built. When the line was completed in 1854, he was the engineer on the first locomotive that pulled a train from Nashville to Chattanooga. The Nashville & Chattanooga created new towns, new wealth and a new corporate landscape as it brought the industrial age to Middle Tennessee.[106] Alexander and his wife, Margaret, lived the rest of their lives in Nashville and are buried in Mount Olivet Cemetery in Nashville.

Alexander's son Robert Tolmie (1844–1872), four years old when the family came to America from Glasgow, moved to Knoxville and became a machinist with the Southern Railway. Tragically, he died in a personal dispute at the rail yard at age twenty-seven. Details of the event appeared in the April 18, 1872 *Knoxville Daily Chronicle*.

Robert's widow, Margaret Anderson Tolmie (1849–1914), also a native of Glasgow, was left with their two-year-old son, Andrew McMurry Tolmie (1870–1951). Margaret remarried in 1876 to Joseph Armbruster (1831–1906), a native of Stuttgart, Germany. Joseph was a master car builder with the East Tennessee, Virginia and Georgia Railway and later a traveling inspector for the Southern Railway. They had two children, Mary and Joseph Armbruster.

Southern Railway Depot. Detroit Publishing Company. "Southern Railway Station, Knoxville, Tenn [Between 1900 and 1906]." *Library of Congress.*

Andrew Tolmie also became a machinist with the Southern Railway. In 1891, he married Annie Atkin Howell

(1872–1955), a native of Chattanooga and the great-great-granddaughter of Tennessee governor John Sevier, and they had seven children. Annie served as a voting registrar for decades and was active in the Order of the Eastern Star until her death.

The golden age of railroading lasted from roughly 1880 through the 1920s. Even into the 1930s, the *Knoxville News Sentinel* pages were full of news of the "railroad men," their doings, opinions and memorial services. When the Railroad Retirement Act was passed in 1939, providing monthly annuities based on age and service or disability, the July 4 *News Sentinel* devoted the front page to the seventy-five local railroad men who were retiring, some in their seventies and one who was eighty-three. The article stated that the army of retirees nationwide had swelled to fifty-five thousand. Andrew Tolmie, age sixty-seven, was one of the eleven men pictured. He said that, even though he was retiring, he would still keep an eye on the railroading game, as his two sons also worked for Southern.

The Tolmies are reminders that the pre-1850s Knoxville population consisted primarily of European American Protestants (of mostly English, Scots-Irish or German descent) and a small community of free Blacks and enslaved persons. By the mid-1850s, large numbers of Irish Catholics had arrived. Many of these new citizens found work on the railroads. As Jack Neely stated in a Knoxville History post, "Refugees Helped Create Knoxville as We Know It": "Knoxville's first railroads, the East TN and GA and the East TN and VA, were under construction just as Irish were arriving. It was difficult, dangerous work, laying steel rails through mountains and across rivers, that other Americans avoided."

In 1941, Andrew and two other retired Coster Shop employees attended the 1941 inauguration of President Franklin Roosevelt. In 1950, at age eighty, Andrew was elected treasurer of the local Lodge No. 58 of the Association of Machinists, the fiftieth consecutive year he had been elected to that post. He was also a fifty-year member of the Masonic Temple, and both he and Annie had been past presidents of the Machinists Auxiliary.[107] During those years, he attended many union conventions and visited his two daughters in D.C., riding the trains he had worked on. Andrew died a year later, just two months shy of his eighty-first birthday. Annie died in 1954.

Andrew, at the half-century mark, was witnessing the end of an era. The last steam locomotive pulled into Knoxville's Southern Depot in June 1953; thereafter, rail was fueled by diesel. Passenger rail miles peaked in the mid-1940s, then dropped by half between 1951 and 1960 and half again between 1961 and 1970. In 1970, President Richard Nixon signed into law the Rail Passenger Service Act (Public Law 91-518), relieving the nation's railroads of the requirement that they continue passenger service.[108] That year saw the last passenger train through Knoxville, an overnighter from Birmingham to D.C. around August 1970. That last steam locomotive in 1953, no. 154, was preserved and put on display at Chilhowee Park. In 2008, it was restored for service as the Three Rivers Rambler, a short excursion line along the Tennessee River to a point where the Holston, French Broad and Tennessee Rivers join.[109]

ELIZA M. WASHBURN

Often, the most elusive biographies are the most intriguing; and, often, especially in the nineteenth century and earlier, the most elusive are of women. Eliza Jane (1844–1928) lived an interesting life: from a farm in Arkansas, through the Civil War and the golden age of the Turks Islands, to the postwar modernization of Washington, D.C., and to the seat of the Ottoman Empire, all by the age of thirty. But most of what we know about her comes from what has been written about the men she married, Edward Maynard (1843–1868) and William Parsons Washburn (1830–1904), both of whom are also buried in Old Gray.

The Maynards and Washburns were old New England families. Edward Maynard, Eliza's first love, was the son of Horace Maynard (1814–1882) of Westboro, Massachusetts, and Laura Ann Washburn (1813–1896) of Royalton, Vermont. William Washburn (1830–1904), Eliza'a second husband, was born in Amherst, Massachusetts, to Reverend Royal Washburn and Harriet Parsons Washburn, also natives, respectively, of Massachusetts and Vermont. Laura Maynard, sister of Reverend Washburn, was William Washburn's aunt.

These were Amherst College men. Horace graduated in 1838, and William graduated in 1851. Edward attended for two years (1859–61), but the Civil War preempted his graduation. An interesting side note is that the Washburns and Dickinsons were neighbors in Amherst. William and Emily Dickinson were the same age. When Emily's older brother Austin entered Williston Seminary in Easthampton at age thirteen, twelve-year-old William took over care of the Dickinson chickens.[110] He and Austin were later classmates at Amherst. Austin graduated in 1850, William a year later. Perez Dickinson, Emily's cousin, moved to Knoxville around 1830.

In 1856, Horace persuaded twenty-six-year-old William to relocate to Knoxville to study law. Horace had taught at East Tennessee College (later the University of Tennessee) (1841–43) and had decided to make Knoxville his home after being admitted to the bar in 1844. When the Civil War broke out in 1861, William was at the beginning of his law career in Knoxville. He chose the stance of his adopted city and served in the Confederate army and was soon promoted to colonel. When the war ended, he returned to Knoxville and formed a law partnership with Horace.

Edward Maynard joined the Union army at age eighteen and was quickly promoted to lieutenant colonel with the Sixth Infantry. After the war, he held a minor position for eighteen months under Governor Brownlow in Nashville. In 1865, Edward wrote his father that he intended to marry twenty-year-old Eliza Jane "Lida" Harper of Hamilton, Ohio. They possibly met in 1862–63, when Edward's regiment fought in southern Ohio.

Eliza Jane Harper was the daughter of Mary Jane Hueston Harper of Butler County, Ohio, and Robert Harper, a planter and boatbuilder who was born in County Down, Ireland. Robert immigrated to Baltimore in 1826 or 1827 and then went to Hamilton, Ohio, in 1831. He lived briefly in Arkansas in the mid-1840s and moved back to Ohio. Eliza was born on his farm in Johnson County, Arkansas, on January 17, 1845. Robert Harper was variously a farmer, grocer and "canal collector" (collecting barge fees) on the Miami and Erie Canal, which ran through Hamilton. The Harpers had six daughters. By 1882, according to a history of Butler County[111] of that year, there were only three still living: Hannah (Lawder) in Missouri and Eliza and Kate (Chamberlain) in Knoxville. Both Hannah and Kate died in 1921. Kate is buried in Old Gray. Mary Harper died in 1879, Robert in 1894; they are both buried in Greenwood Cemetery in Hamilton.

On September 12, 1866, three months after their marriage, Edward and Eliza, twenty-three and twenty-one, respectively, sailed for Grand Turk Island in the West Indies, where Edward began his new post as U.S. consul to Turks Islands. On January 10, 1868, Edward, age twenty-five, died there of yellow fever[112] and was buried in the parish churchyard. On February 29, their son Edward Robert Horace Maynard was born. In April 1868, Eliza, "baby Eddie" and a nursemaid sailed for America. In June, Horace's youngest child, James, fifteen, was sent to Turks Island to retrieve the remains of his brother but was informed that local ordinances forbade disinterment for a year after burial. In October 1869, Edward's remains, accompanied by his father, were returned to Knoxville and buried in Gray Cemetery on October 31.

For the next few years, Eliza and Eddie went back and forth between Hamilton and Knoxville. In 1872–73, they spent the winter in Washington, D.C., where Horace was serving in the U.S. House of Representatives. In 1875, they sailed for Europe with Laura and Horace, who was appointed U.S. minister to the Ottoman Empire (1875–80). Eliza and Eddie spent two years in Constantinople and returned to Knoxville in 1877.

On November 3, 1880, after twelve years a widow, Eliza married a second time, to William P. Washburn, by that time a well-known attorney in the Washburn Templeton law firm in Knoxville.[113] William was the nephew of Horace Maynard's wife, Laura Washburn Maynard. The marriage took place at Eliza's aunt's home in Hamilton.[114] Horace, then U.S. postmaster general, and Laura attended. Eliza was thirty-five; William was fifty and had been a widower for sixteen years. He married his first wife, Ruth Marion "Minnie" Brown Leonard, in 1864; she died in 1877 and is buried beside him in Old Gray. In 1885, William and Eliza had a son, William Parsons Washburn Jr. A daughter, Mary, died in childbirth.

William died in 1904 at age seventy-three. Eliza and their son, William Washburn Jr., frequently traveled together, visiting friends and family, and spent the summer of 1908 in Europe. Eliza remained a widow, settling into a suburban life on Kingston Pike and attending social events at Cherokee Country Club. She died in 1928 at age eighty-three and is buried in the Washburn family plot. Edward is buried in the Maynard plot, as is their son Edward "Eddie" Robert Horace Maynard, who died in 1939 at age seventy-one.

ANNA CATHERINE WILEY

Impressionist artist Anna Catherine Wiley (1879–1958), known to family members as Kate, was born in Coal Creek (Lake City/Rocky Top), Anderson County, Tennessee, to Edwin Floyd Wiley and Mary McAdoo. Catherine Wiley played an instrumental role in Knoxville's art community at the beginning of the twentieth century and is ranked among America's premier impressionists. The tragedy is that just as she was gaining national attention, she suffered a "mental breakdown" and was admitted to a psychiatric hospital in Pennsylvania, where she spent the last thirty-two years of her life.

The Wiley family moved from Coal Creek to Laurel Avenue in Knoxville's Fort Sanders area in 1882. Edwin and Mary had seven children. The first four—Edwin, Emma, May and Kate—were born in Rocky Top, and Robert, Noel and John were born in Knoxville.

Educated in the public schools of Knoxville, Catherine enrolled in one of the first classes of women students at the University of Tennessee in 1895. While a student at UT (1895–97), her artistic talent emerged in her illustrations for the college yearbook. Wishing to expand her art training beyond the traditional woman's role of illustrating books, she enrolled in the Art Students League in New York in 1903 and spent a brief period in 1905 at the New York School of Art (formerly the Chase School of Art), where she studied under impressionist William Merritt Chase.

In 1905, Catherine returned to UT to teach art, a discipline that at the time was housed within the School of Home Economics. During her tenure (1905–18), she drew many illustrations for the *Volunteer*, the university's yearbook, and helped to shape UT's art program into one of the best in the South. She was also becoming a major figure in Knoxville's Nicholson Art League, the leading group of Knoxville artists during the first quarter of the twentieth century. As a member and 1913 president of the league, she participated in a number of exhibitions and won the award for Most Meritorious Collection at the 1910 Appalachian Exposition in Knoxville. She

Top: Anna Catherine Wiley. *McClung Historical Collection, Knox County Public Library*.

Bottom: Lloyd Branson. *McClung Historical Collection, Knox County Public Library*.

continued to receive art instruction from Lloyd Branson, one of the most influential leaders in Knoxville's art circle, and spent summers studying art in the Northeast with major American impressionists, such as Robert Reid, Jonas Lie and Martha Walter.

Wiley continued to achieve success and acclaim during her career for her influence and recognition across the South. Striving to break regional boundaries, she also chaired the Fine Arts Department for the National Conservation Exposition in Knoxville in 1913 and exhibited in the 1910s and 1920s at major venues across the nation, including the Pennsylvania Academy of Fine Arts (PAFA) (1913), the National Academy of Design (1915) and the Cincinnati Art Museum. Her presence in these national exhibitions helped draw attention and notoriety to southern women artists. After seeing the PAFA exhibit, a French magazine of art and letters wrote from Paris to see if they might do a story on her. "She stated that she would allow them to reproduce some of her paintings as they requested,"[115] but it is unknown if that ever happened. In 1917, Catherine was named best painter at several Tennessee exhibitions and received the award for Best Southern Artist at the Southwestern Fair in Atlanta.

In June 1925, Catherine's oil landscape *By the Arbor* won the grand prize at the Nashville Art Association's exhibit at the Carnegie library. The June 28 *Nashville Banner* stated, "Miss Wiley, who is one of the South's finest artists, has won distinction for her masterly handling of figures outdoors." June 1925 saw the death of her mentor, Lloyd Branson. This loss, combined with the death of her father in 1919, caused Catherine to suffer a "mental breakdown."[116] But most Wiley historians fail to take into account the sudden death of her older brother Edwin in October 1924.

Edwin C. Wiley, the first child born in Coal Creek in 1872, seven years her senior, was a scholar, educator and librarian. He received his BA and MA at UT; taught English at UT, Vanderbilt and the University of California; and earned a PhD in philosophy at George Washington University. He was the first paid librarian at UT and was the librarian at the Library of Congress in D.C. (1906–13); at UC Berkeley (1913–15); at the U.S. Naval War College (1916–22) in Newport, Rhode Island; and, at the time of his death, the public library of Peoria, Illinois. He was fluent in several languages. His wife, Garnet Noel of Nashville, was a published poet and a teacher in Peoria.

Catherine and her brother had shared aesthetic interests and ambitions, for Edwin was also an art scholar. In 1903, he published *The Old and the New Renaissance: A Group of Studies in Arts and Letters.* The *Nashville Banner* reviewer wrote: "Mr. Wiley's essays reveal a thorough acquaintance with his subject, genuine artistic insight, and an original line of thought....His style is clear and excellent, and many passages of the essays possess true literary beauty."[117] Edwin, according to his obituary, had been in ill health for a year and had "been stricken suddenly at home."

Catherine's two unmarried sisters, Eleanor "Nell," also an artist, and May, with whom Anna lived at 1317 White Avenue, were unable to care for her and, in 1926 quietly committed her to Norristown State Hospital near Philadelphia, a long-term psychiatric facility established in 1880 and still in operation. She was forty-seven and remained hospitalized there until her death in 1958. To the best of our knowledge, Catherine never painted again. According to the 1930 census, her younger brothers Ernest and Noel were living in Philadelphia and, according to her obituary, still lived there in 1958.

Catherine's artistic legacy is secure. Her untitled mother-and-child painting (1913) sold at auction in 2012 to the Knoxville Museum of Art for $107,900. Her painting *Willow Pond* (1914) hangs in the Metropolitan Museum of Art. The Calvin M. McClung Historical Collection (a division of the Knox County Public Library system) owns the largest collection of Wiley's works, with more than three dozen paintings, about a dozen drawings and her scrapbooks. In 2021, Catherine's grandnephew, the late Edwin P. Wiley, donated three of her paintings to the Knoxville Museum of Art. Her work can be seen in the KMA's collection Higher Ground: A Century of the Visual Arts in East Tennessee.

MAY LAWSON MCGHEE WILLIAMS

Lawson (1860–1883) was born on a five-thousand-acre plantation on the Little Tennessee River in Monroe County, Tennessee. The second of five daughters born to Charles McClung McGhee (1828–1907) and Cornelia White McGhee (1836–1903), Lawson preferred her second given name, which was the maiden name of her great-great-grandmother Mary Lawson White, wife of James White, founder of Knoxville. Cornelia was McGhee's second wife; his first was Cornelia's sister Isabella, who died in childbirth along with their infant son just eleven months after their marriage.

By the time Lawson was a year or so old, the McGhee family had moved to Knoxville, where May's father began amassing wealth through a variety of investments—land, cattle, coal and, primarily, railroads. In 1872, McGhee built a mansion at 505 Locust Street to house his growing family. The house, designed by Joseph Baumann, was Second Empire in style, had fourteen large rooms and was described as a "palatial mansion." It sat on the crest of a hill a few blocks from Knoxville's business district, and the yard and gardens covered a full city block. There, Cornelia entertained on a grand scale. When President Rutherford B. Hayes toured the South in 1877, the McGhees hosted a reception for six hundred people, many of whom walked through the house to shake Hayes's hand. Many stayed to wander the grounds, ablaze in gaslights, or dance on a garden platform said to accommodate one hundred couples.

Lawson was not a great beauty, but as her obituary stated, "Her refined and charming manners and amiable disposition made her a favorite, and she was greatly beloved by a wide circle of friends."[118] Lawson and her sisters attended the Ward Seminary for Young Ladies, a prestigious "finishing school" in Nashville. In 1870, the Educational Bureau in Washington, D.C., ranked Ward Seminary among the top three educational institutions for women in the nation. In June 1875, sixteen-year-old Lawson, her eighteen-year-old sister Margie and two other Ward students sailed for Europe on the steamer *City of Berlin*. They were accompanied by Dr. William Ward, the seminary founder.[119]

May did charity work, teaching at the St. Luke's Mission School on Vine Avenue and, of course, enjoyed a busy social life not only in Knoxville, Nashville and Chattanooga but also in New York City, which she and her family visited often. Over the years, her father had formed many business connections there and belonged to at least three city clubs.

On October 20, 1881, Lawson married New Orleans native David Shelby Williams, who was then a practicing attorney in Nashville. The wedding took place at Everett House in New York City. Less than two years later, Lawson died in childbirth, and the infant daughter died a couple of weeks later.

In 1885, McGhee funded a $50,000 public library as a memorial to his beloved daughter. The original library occupied what is now the Rebori Building on the corner of Vine and Gay. A major fire gutted the building in 1904 and forced the library to relocate temporarily to rented space. In 1917, the library reopened in a marble structure at the corner of Market Street and Commerce Avenue, where it remained until the present library on Clinch Avenue was built in 1971. Lawson McGhee Library is the oldest continuously operating library in the state.

Charles McGhee died of pneumonia in his bedroom in the spring of 1907. The last of the McGhee family to occupy the house on Locust was Margaret "Margie" White McGhee and her husband, George Baxter. In 1916, the Freemasons acquired his house and, except for a couple of rooms, radically remodeled it and simplified and consolidated its Victorian flourishes for new use as the organization's secretive temple, a purpose it has served ever since. The same year, Masonic Court (now known as Kendrick Place) was built on the north side of it, and in 1929, the YMCA was built on the south side.

NANCY ISABELLE COFFIN WILLIAMS

As William Faulkner famously said, "The past is never dead. It's not even past." Nowhere is that statement more evident than during an international pandemic. An Old Gray Cemetery story from the end of the nineteenth century that resonates with the current experience of quarantining due to the coronavirus pandemic is about Tennessee Williams's paternal grandmother, Nancy Isabelle "Belle" Coffin Williams (1853–1884).

Belle was born on May 15, 1853, in Greeneville, Tennessee, to Cornelius Coffin and Nancy McCorkle. In 1874, Belle married Thomas Lanier Williams, a young Knoxville lawyer. The 1880 U.S. Census shows Belle, Thomas and their two children, Ella and Cornelius (Tennessee's father), living at 24 West Clinch Avenue downtown.

Sometime in the next few years, Belle contracted tuberculosis. In September 1884, she and Thomas traveled to San Antonio, Texas, in search of a cure. Conventional wisdom of the day had it that the best thing for consumption, as tuberculosis was called then, was to seek a drier climate. "Lungers," as tuberculars were called, traveled to Texas by ship and train, heading to high and drier country in Central and West Texas. San Antonio, a popular destination after the coming of the railroad there in 1877, was often touted in eastern newspapers as the "Sanitarium of the West." Josiah Gregg, native Tennessean, trader and naturalist (*Commerce of the Prairies*, 1844), praised the "salubrity of the climate [in]…New Mexico. Nowhere—not even under the much-boasted Sicilian skies…can a purer or a more wholesome atmosphere be found. Bilious diseases—the great scourge of the valley of the Mississippi—are here almost unknown."

Several East Tennesseans had already settled in Texas, and local newspapers often carried long, detailed travel accounts of train journeys and stays there extolling the climate and landscape, the exotic culture and cuisine and the beauty of historic mission towns along the San Antonio River. One such letter from an East Tennessean identified as J.R.P. in the August 1876 issue of the *Morristown Gazette* reads:

We come now to speak of our trip from Galveston to "San Anton," as the Texans lovingly call the old town; where consumptives have for years been coming, apparently upon their last legs, only to find renewed life and vigor. It would be an idle task for us to attempt to give you an adequate ideal of this beautiful country situated between the Colorado and the Rio Grande, in the midst of which section is situated the ancient city of San Antonio, a place thoroughly European in aspect, and may be termed the "Pearl of Texas."…

Our letter is already too long to allow us to speak of other curiosities in and around San Antonio. If time would permit, and the patience of your readers would not be exhausted, I would speak of the plazas, pretty residences, charming lawns, and lovely gardens, as well as the San Antonio and San Pedro Rivers, fed from a thousand sweet springs, which arise as if by magic, and gush forth from the beautiful Guadalupe Mountains, forming these two beautiful rivers running through the town's center, a perpetual delight and a constant treasure.

The train trip must have been an arduous weeks-long journey—dust, heat and coal fumes—for someone with a respiratory disease, but hope outweighed discomfort. The route would have been Knoxville–Chattanooga–Nashville–Memphis, then possibly a mail boat from Memphis to St. Louis; rail again on the route St. Louis–Little Rock–Dallas–Houston–Galveston–San Antonio. The October 6, 1884 *San Antonio Light* announced that prominent Knoxville lawyer T.L. Williams and his wife were at the Vance House, a two-story hotel near the Alamo Plaza. Vance House, originally the sixteen-room Greek Revival mansion built in 1859 for banker James Vance of Strabane, Ireland, was turned into an elegant hostelry in 1872. Thanks to the railroad, the city was enjoying a bustling popularity and booming urbanism. The population of the city more than doubled, from twenty thousand in 1880 to forty thousand by 1890. Many of the streets were still unpaved, but for five cents, passengers could ride the horse- or mule-drawn omnibuses from the depot to the hotel. The Vance room rate was two dollars a day, with reduced rates by the week or by the month.

Like most American cities of that era, San Antonio, despite the glowing accolades in eastern newspapers, was not without disease. In addition to poor sanitation, the two rivers, the San Antonio and the San Pedro, flooded almost annually, bringing various epidemics. In 1866, a major cholera epidemic claimed many lives over three years; in 1869, there were outbreaks of dysentery and typhoid fever; 1879 saw a tuberculosis epidemic; and, between 1866 and 1903, there were localized epidemics of yellow fever. As is true throughout history, the poorest communities—in Texas, these were populated by African Americans, Mexicans and American Indians—were the hardest hit by epidemics. The Indigenous peoples had no immunity to European diseases. A 1973 article by Smithsonian research anthropologist John C. Ewers identified no fewer than thirty major epidemics—mainly of smallpox and cholera—between 1528 and 1890 that wiped out perhaps 95 percent of Texas Indians.[120]

By midcentury, doctors educated in some of Europe's finest medical schools had begun arriving in Texas and implementing their progressive ideas. Most important among those pioneer physicians was Dr. Ferdinand Herff of Germany, whose long practice in San Antonio spanned sixty years (1850–1912). Trained as a surgeon in the universities of Bonn, Berlin and Giessen, in San Antonio he became a general practitioner, seeing patients in their homes or in hotels and sometimes operating on dining tables or in carriages. Unlike U.S.-trained physicians, Herff was a stickler for cleanliness—he washed his hands and filtered and boiled water to be used in surgery. In 1853, he was one of the founders of the Texas State Medical Association and served on the Texas Board of Medical Examiners.[121]

The biggest development came with the arrival of members of the Sisters of Charity of the Incarnate Word from Lyon, France. The newly arrived French Catholic bishop in Galveston, Claude Dubuis, witnessing the devastation of recent cholera and yellow fever epidemics, was appalled at the lack of medical facilities and called on the Lyon order to send nuns. Three nuns were chosen, trained and sent across the ocean. They soon opened Galveston's Charity Hospital, the first Catholic hospital in Texas. The nuns were then called to the frontier town of San Antonio to establish a hospital there. After a dusty, three-week trip by stagecoach, the nuns were met with the news that their designated building, an old renovated church, had been lost to fire. With the help of Dr. Herff, they set about fashioning a hospital, chapel and convent from a surviving two-story adobe structure. After eight months of arduous labor, Santa Rosa Infirmary opened on December 3, 1869, with a public announcement, to the displeasure of some, that the hospital would be open "to all persons without distinction of nationality or creed" or ability to pay. Santa Rosa Infirmary became Santa Rosa Hospital. Dr. Herff served as the first dean of the nuns' nursing school, which opened in 1903. Today, the Christus Santa Rosa Health System, operating five hospitals on four campuses and several specialty clinics, is the only faith-based, not-for-profit healthcare system in San Antonio.

Except for tuberculosis, the year 1884 was relatively disease-free in San Antonio. Starting in 1870, the city had begun sanitation improvements; and public authorities developed stable institutions for supervising sanitation, water sources and food inspection. And although quarantining was practiced in Texas port cities, most of inland Texas was more engaged in quarantining cattle against Texas cattle fever. Quarantining was not strictly enforced in San Antonio until 1912, when the Bexar County Tuberculosis Sanatorium opened.

We don't know if Belle enjoyed any of her time in San Antonio before her disease grew too advanced—was she able to take a surrey ride along San Pedro Springs Park, lounge on the Vance House balcony or have a meal in the dining room? We don't know what kind of medical services or assistance she had. It is likely that Dr. Herff and/or one of the Santa Rosa nuns was summoned. The October 15, 1884 *San Antonio Light* reported that she died at Vance House the previous night, that she had come to San Antonio about twenty days earlier hoping to regain her strength. The *Light* published notices of other deaths from consumption that year, some of which also took place at Vance House. The October 6 edition reported the suicide by poison of a former clerk at the Vance who had given up his job due to an advanced stage of consumption. Belle was thirty-one years old, had been married only ten years and left three young children back in Knoxville: five-year-old Cornelius (Tennessee's father), nine-year-old Ella and baby Isabel, fourteen months.

Thomas accompanied his wife's body back to Knoxville, where she was buried in Old Gray. He did not remarry. The 1900 U.S. Census shows him living at the Tulane Hotel in Nashville with Ella, Cornelius and Isabel. He had made two unsuccessful runs for the governorship and was still Tennessee commissioner of railroads. He died in 1908 at age fifty-nine and is buried alongside Belle, their three children, his grandparents and four siblings.

Tuberculosis deaths in America continued until a vaccine became available in 1921. Sporadic cases occurred over the years, but there were no serious outbreaks in the United States until the late 1980s, when a major resurgence was attributed to the elimination of public health facilities in New York and the emergence of HIV. In 1993, the World Health Organization (WHO) issued a declaration of a global health emergency due to TB; and every year, nearly half a million new cases of multidrug-resistant tuberculosis (MDR-TB) are estimated to occur worldwide. In May 2020, the WHO issued a memo that states, "Between 2020 and 2025 an additional 1.4 million TB deaths could be registered as direct consequence of the COVID-19 pandemic." Many medical and public health advances have been made since Belle's death, but many of the same challenges still exist. The past, as Faulkner said, will always be with us.

DELLA DAISY YOE

Della Yoe (1874–1963) is another little-known writer buried in Old Gray. Della was a journalist when very few women worked for newspapers. She was born in Mossy Creek, Jefferson County, Tennessee, to John Williams Yoe (1842–1895) and Ann Eliza Meek (1844–1926). John Yoe practiced law there, and in 1882, the family moved to Clinch Avenue in the area then known as West Knoxville (now known as Fort Sanders). When that area was incorporated as the City of West Knoxville in 1888, John Yoe became the first mayor, a position he held until his death. John and Ann had three daughters and a son. One of the daughters, Alice Fay, married Harry Pearle Ijams, ornithologist and illustrator, and their twenty-acre bird sanctuary along the Tennessee River evolved into Ijams Nature Center.

Della graduated from the University of Tennessee in 1897 with a double major in Latin and sciences. She also took a Saturday class for teachers at UT (1903–4), but we find no evidence that she ever taught school. John Yoe died unexpectedly in 1905, just two weeks before Della's twenty-first birthday. After John's death, Della and her mother moved into an apartment in the Anderson Flats on Union Avenue, then to Hill Avenue and Locust and, in 1914, the Priscilla on Walnut.

Della's first job was with the *Knoxville Journal and Tribune* as a suburban (West Knoxville) reporter. Being a journalist at that time was still a fairly radical career choice for a woman. Until then, there had been only one female reporter in Knoxville, Pattie Boyd, the society columnist for the *Knoxville Tribune*, later to merge with the *Knoxville Journal*. Lucy Curtis Templeton was a proofreader and telegraph editor with the *Knoxville Sentinel* but would not become a regular staffer with her own column until 1926.[122]

In 1915, one of Della's assignments was to interview actor Charles Coburn,[123] director of the Coburn Players, who were in town performing *Macbeth*.[124] The interview spurred an interesting pause in Della's writing career. Coburn had been in Knoxville years before as a performer in summer stock. In 1902, he began a two-year residency at Staub's Theatre on Gay Street. It was in Knoxville that he met his future wife, Ivah Wills,[125] who shared his love of Shakespeare. They married in 1906 and formed the Coburn Players, a touring repertory company that presented Shakespeare, French and Greek dramas and comedies at college campuses throughout the United States. They performed for five or six seasons under the auspices of UT. One of the last performances there was *Macbeth*. The interview sparked a lifelong friendship between Charles, Ivah and Della. Della quit her job at the *Journal*, joined the road show and, for a brief period, played several bit parts and served as the publicity agent for the group.

In much of her writing, Della championed accomplished and enterprising women. In 1916, she interviewed Helen Keller, who was on tour lecturing at the Bijou.[126] In 1935, she wrote about women who had created mountain retreats without the help of men.[127] In 1932, she wrote about Mrs. Orin Turner (former Knoxvillian Lavinia Morrison), who founded a successful nursery and floral service in Statesville, North Carolina, Park Place Greenhouses.[128]

By 1917, Della was in charge of the woman's page of the *Charlotte News and Observer*, covering everything from the Red Cross, city and county food administrators, the YWCA, city schools and teachers, to city and county boards of education. She resigned a year later to join the Community War Camp Service.[129] She worked for several months for the War Camp in Charlotte, then was transferred to Fayetteville, North Carolina, in 1919, and to Milwaukee, Wisconsin, in 1920. Around 1921, she returned to New York, where she became head correspondent for a Swiss company that imported textiles. She lived in New York City for sixteen years, during which she was keen on disabusing many of her fellow New Yorkers of their stereotypical opinion of Appalachian mountaineers.[130] Following the stock market crash, she held a variety of temporary jobs and then returned to Knoxville and became the receptionist at the Audigier Gallery in UT's Hoskins Library.[131]

While at UT, she began conducting interviews for the Federal Writers' Project (FWP), the results of which would become her lasting achievement. The FWP was created in 1935 as part of the U.S. Works Progress Administration (WPA) to provide employment for historians, teachers, writers, librarians and other white-collar workers. In the Depression years between 1936 and 1938, the FWP sent out-of-work writers in seventeen states to interview ordinary people in order to document their life stories. At its peak, the FWP employed about 6,500 men and women across the country, paying them a subsistence wage of about twenty dollars a week. Four hundred interviews reflecting the lives of real people selected from among whites and Blacks in three basic fields of work in the South—farm laborers and owners, factory and mill workers and people engaged in service occupations—and those on relief were submitted. Of those four hundred interviews, thirty-seven were selected for the collection *These Are Our Lives*, published by the University of North Carolina in 1939. Of the fourteen from Tennessee, four were written by Della Yoe.

Della also participated in the FWP's Slave Narratives Project, which resulted in seventeen bound volumes published in 1941 and titled *Slave Narratives: A Folk History of Slavery in the United States from Interviews with Former Slaves*. Two-thirds of the people interviewed were over eighty. Her twenty-six interviews, conducted in Knoxville and Nashville, comprise Volume 15, *Tennessee Slave Narratives*. In Knoxville, the interviews were conducted in the old YMCA, which from 1906 to 1930 was located in the old Palace Hotel building at the corner of State and Commerce. In an era before recording devices, Della did a remarkable job of capturing the phonetic dialogue. All of these narratives are available on the Library of Congress website.

Della loved the mountains of North Carolina and Tennessee and wrote about them eloquently. In 1939, she wrote a series of thumbnail sketches of the various communities comprising Campbell County, Tennessee. These sketches were published in the *Lafollette (TN) Press* during Tennessee Homecoming 1986. Well into the 1940s, Della had regular articles in the *Knoxville News Sentinel* about Elkmont, where she spent many summer days, hiking with friends or attending club meetings at the Wonderland Hotel.

Della was popular, and her doings appeared frequently in the society pages as she traveled near and far visiting friends and being visited. She was in a number of local clubs, such as the Knoxville Women's Auxiliary of the International Typographical Union (a labor organization for newspaper workers), the YWCA, the Tennessee Women's Press and Author's Club (which elected her corresponding secretary in 1914), the Knoxville chapter of the World Caravan Guild and the American League of Pen Women. One wonders how she had time to write and publish so much.

In 1948, *Knoxville News Sentinel* columnist Lucy Templeton invited Della to contribute reminiscences of "West Knoxville," the old neighborhood of Yoe's youth—Clinch, Laurel, Highland, White and Tenth-Fifteenth—an area now known as Fort Sanders. The Sunday series began on December 5, 1948, and continued through February 20, 1949. These evocative articles recall the residential area as it looked in the late 1880s, when the UT campus consisted of just a few buildings clustered around "The Hill" across Cumberland. There were a few university professors and administrators living there, but mostly the stately homes were built by

Knoxville's growing upper and middle classes—politicians, merchants, industrialists and other professionals.

Moving block by block, Della described the houses, lawns and families with old Knoxville names like Cowan, Maynard, Briscoe, Flenniken, Ross, Ijams and Luttrell. There was only one sidewalk, which was plank and extended along Clinch. Almost everyone, she said, owned a horse and carriage. A mule-drawn "hack" with tinkling bells on the harness served as public transportation until replaced by a trolley. She attended West Knoxville School (later, Van Gilder School) on the corner of Thirteenth and Highland Avenue. On summer evenings, her favorite teacher, Anna Morris, would lead the children up to the "old fort" (the site of the Battle of Fort Sanders), between Fifteenth and Eighteenth, for "astronomical observations." Cannon placements remained visible for many years, and in summer, the old entrenchments were covered in daisies. The battle site was known as "the Commons" and provided a natural amphitheater that served as picnic grounds for churches, schools and private groups, as well as fireworks displays on the Fourth of July. A pine woodland extended from the slopes down to Third Creek and a pond that supplied water for the Knoxville Iron Company and that "had all the elements of a natural lake," with colonies of water lilies and tulip trees shading the banks.

Della retired from UT in 1959 after almost two decades at the Audigier Gallery and moved into Asbury Acres, Holston Conference United Methodist Church Home for the Aged in Maryville, Tennessee. She died there on Christmas Eve in 1963 at age eighty-seven. The Knoxville she grew up in had disappeared. The old Van Gilder Elementary School, built in 1887, where she had been one of eight students to make the first honor roll, was torn down in 1960. White Avenue had become UT student housing. The old market house built downtown in 1889 was torn down in 1961 to make room for a mall. Conditions for women in the workforce had changed considerably and would change even more with the 1963 Equal Pay Act. Della's job titles at the UT gallery say it all. When she started, her title had been "receptionist"; she called herself "hostess"; her obituary called her "the former curator of the Audigier Gallery, a writer of considerable literary talent."

Della's parents are also buried in Old Gray. Her younger sister Alice Fay and Alice's husband, Harry, are buried in Highland Memorial Cemetery. Her brother John Ernest Yoe is buried in Mount Hope Cemetery in Franklin, Tennessee, and her older sister Lora Lee Yoe Patton is buried in Spring Hill Cemetery in Nashville.

NOTES

Part I

1. Betsey Creekmore, "Nancy Dickinson Estabrook Diary," Special Collections and University Archives, University of Tennessee.
2. *Knoxville (TN) Register*, April 3, 1850.
3. Rule, *Standard History of Knoxville, Tennessee*.
4. "Ravages of Time Faced by Historic Cemetery," *Knoxville (TN) Journal*, October 27, 1949.
5. Thomas Gray, "Elegy Written in a Country Churchyard," 1751.
6. "Mount Auburn Consecrated," Mount Auburn Cemetery, December 8, 2011.
7. "Books for the Holydays," *Daily Nashville (TN) Union*, December 15–20, 1848.
8. "List of Rural Cemeteries in the United States," Wikipedia.
9. Peggy Levy, "Knoxville First Hospital Listed," *Knoxville Journal*, April 26, 1936, 14.
10. Scores of Visitors at the New Hospital Yesterday," *Knoxville (TN) Journal and Tribune*, April 21, 1902.
11. "Knoxville in Sorrow, Buries Its Dead," *Knoxville (TN) Sentinel*, September 26, 1904.
12. Felix von Vondracek, "The Rise of Fraternal Organizations in the United States, 1868–1900," *Social Science* 47, no. 1 (Winter 1972): 26–33.

Part II

13. "Henry B. Wetzell," in *East Tennessee: Historical and Biographical* (Chattanooga, TN: A.D. Smith, 1893), 91–2.

14. Doman, Katherine Hoffman, "Setting the Record Straight: Anne W. Armstrong, Regionalism, and the Social Efficacy of Fiction" (PhD dissertation, University of Tennessee, 2008).

15. "R. Armstrong to Be Buried at Big Creek," *Bristol (TN) News Bulletin*, March 25, 1931, 7.

16. "Crescent Bluff, Once, Handsome Kingston Pike Residence, Now Smouldering Ruin," *Knoxville Journal and Tribune*, May 5, 1911, 7.

17. "$75,000 Campaign for Melrose Center to Open," *Knoxville (TN) News Sentinel*, February 23, 1930, 2.

18. "Depression Gave Art Setback Here, Causing Abandonment of Melrose Center," *Knoxville Journal*, June 4, 1933, 43.

19. "Workers Convert Melrose into Apartment House," *Knoxville News Sentinel*, August 21, 1932, 18.

20. "Mrs. Eleanor Deane Audigier Dies in Rome," *Knoxville Journal*, August 30, 1931, 2.

21. "Death of Mrs. L.B. Audigier Robs Knoxville of Foremost Art Patron," *Knoxville Journal*, August 30, 1931, 4.

22. "Mrs. L.B. Audigier Writes of War Relief Work in Rome, Italy," *Knoxville Sentinel*, October 6, 1916, 6.

23. "Capt. F.C. Beaman Dies at Age 75," *Knoxville Sentinel*, August 19, 1911, 6.

24. "Three Young People Meet a Violent Death Picnicing Near Knoxville," *Morristown (TN) Gazette*, August 5, 1896, 3.

25. "Mrs. Barry Rites Today," *Knoxville Journal*, August 21, 1955, 27.

26. Zollie Howard, "'Are Women Three Times as Poetical as Men?' Queries Book of Verse Reviewer," *Knoxville News Sentinel*, September 24, 1939.

27. "Philathea, Philathea," in *The Official Hymnal of the World-wide Baraca and Philathea Union*, hymn no. 34, subtitled "The Philathea Class Song of First Baptist Church, Knoxville, Tenn." (Syracuse, NY: Baraca Supply, 1908), 134.

28. Marshall Alonze Hudson and Henrietta Heron. *The Philathea Bible Class: The Story of a Movement for Women; What It Means, How It Works, the Secret Service, the Constitution, the Teacher* (Syracuse, NY: Baraca and Philathea Supply Co., 1914).

29. W.B. Lenoir, *History of Sweetwater Valley*, c. 1916, 249. Hathi Trust. www.hathitrust.org.

30. Alesha Shumar, "Pride of the Southland: A Look Back at 150 Years of UT's Marching Band," University of Tennessee Libraries, August 20, 2019.

31. Rob Simpson, "Thomas 'Blind Tom' Wiggins." New Georgia Encyclopedia, last modified July 9, 2018. www.newgeorgiaencyclopedia.org.

32. *Evening Sentinel* (Knoxville, TN), January 29, 1890, 1, and *London County Record*, January 30, 1980, 8.

33. *The Heritage of Cleveland County* (Shelby, NC: Cleveland County Historical Association, 1982), 661.

34. *Knoxville News Sentinel*, April 29, 1927.

35. *Southern Journal of Homeopathy* (April 1997–March 1998).

36. Transactions of the 54th Session of the American Homeopathic Society, Omaha, Nebraska, June 23, 1898.

37. Betsey Creekmore, "World War I—Students' Army Training Corps," Volopedia, 2018, University of Tennessee Libraries, https://volumes.lib.utk.edu/news/volopedia-encyclopedia-of-ut-history-and-traditions-now-online.

38. Jack Neely, "The Spanish Flu: How 1918 Was the Same but Very Different," Knoxville History Project, April 3, 2020, www.knoxvillehistoryproject.org.

39. *Knoxville Journal and Tribune*, September 13, 1901.

40. *Knoxville News Sentinel*, October 15, 1923.

41. Online text of *The Embassy Ball* (377 pp., 1897 ed.) is available at Hathi Trust Digital Library. www.hathitrust.org.

42. *Knoxville Journal and Tribune*, January 20, 1896.

43. Ibid., December 13, 1901.

44. *Knoxville Sentinel*, June 20, 1903.

45. "Guard Against Return of Flu," *Knoxville Sentinel*, October 13, 1919.

46. "Dr. Charles H. Davis (obituary)," *Knoxville Sentinel*, October 22, 1918.

47. Betsey Creekmore, "Perez Dickinson," Volopedia, University of Tennessee Libraries, https://volumes.lib.utk.edu/news/volopedia-encyclopedia-of-ut-history-and-traditions-now-online.

48. "Beautiful Island Home Farm Was Col Dickinson's Pride," *Knoxville Journal*, July 17, 1901.

49. Carol Damon Andrews, "Thinking Musically, Writing Expectantly: New Biographical Information about Emily Dickinson," *New England Quarterly* 81, no. 2 (June 2008): 330–40.

50. Ibid.

51. Ann Bennett, "Island Home Park Historic District," National Register of Historic Places, National Park Service, 1994, www.nps.gov.

52. "Beautiful Island Home Farm Was Col Dickinson's Pride," *Knoxville Journal*, July 17, 1901.
53. David Babelay, "Swiss Settlers, Knoxville," Tennessee Encyclopedia, Tennessee Historical Society, www.tennesseeencyclopedia.net.
54. Aaron Astor, "The Switzerland of America," *New York Times*, June 7, 2011.
55. *Knoxville Journal and Tribune*, May 25, 1909.
56. "Alfred Jules Mercier," My Heritage, www.myheritage.com.
57. "Scotch Educator Is a Visitor in Knoxville," *Knoxville Sentinel*, April 4, 1906.
58. *Knoxville Journal*, November 23, 1935.
59. "Defibaugh-Duenner," *Knoxville News Sentinel*, November 21, 1907.
60. "KHS of 1905 Has Big Part in O'Neill Film," *Knoxville News-Sentinel*, March 5, 1936, 2.
61. John Lynn Ebaugh, comp., *John Jacob Ebaugh, the First "Ebaugh" in America: History of A Maryland Family* (Baltimore, MD: self-published, 1941).
62. "Mrs. Parker Dies, Recalled Civil War," *Knoxville News-Sentinel*, June 15, 1956, 5.
63. *Knoxville (TN) Daily Chronicle*, December 28, 1979, 4.
64. "Mrs. French Dies with Her Task Unfinished," *Knoxville-News Sentinel*, May 15, 1926, 1.
65. "Confederate Hero Answers Summons: Col. James L. Gaines Passes Away at a Nashville Infirmary," *Chattanooga News*, September 30, 1910.
66. *Cairo (IL) Bulletin*, September 24, 1904, and *Daily Review* (Decatur, IL), September 25, 1904.
67. *Knoxville Journal*, April 22, 1929, 37. *Belles Truches*: The Belles Truches flats (or apartments) were erected by Mrs. Adele Esperandieu Brownlow. "The name of the building always excited comment, and, at one time, having the opportunity to ask one of the family connection, Col. Charles Ducloux, the occasion of the name, he said the family in Switzerland had a castle on one of the Swiss lakes, the water so clear and the fish so remarkably visible, the place bore the name *Belles Truches*, beautiful fish, and the name was given in memory of Mrs. Brownlow's ancestral home."
68. "Henry R. Gibson Praises GOP and Recalls Old Days," *Knoxville News Sentinel*, February 13, 1932.
69. "Obituary," *Knoxville News Sentinel*, May 26, 1938, 1.
70. Betsey Creekmore, "Martha Caroline Badgett Henson," Volopedia, University of Tennessee Libraries, https://volumes.lib.utk.edu/news/volopedia-encyclopedia-of-ut-history-and-traditions-now-online.

71. Ibid.
72. Alexander Hynds, "Early Struggles of Frances H. Burnett," *Knoxville Sentinel*, April 1, 1904, 14.
73. Ibid.
74. "John Hodgson Died Last Night," *Knoxville Sentinel*, November 10, 1904, 9.
75. Hynds, "Early Struggles of Frances H. Burnett."
76. *Knoxville Journal and Tribune*, December 16, 1900, 13.
77. Presbyterian Heritage Center, Biographical Index of U.S. Missionaries to China 1900–1920, www.phcmontreat.org.
78. "Miss Rida Jourolmon, One of Knoxville's Most Beloved Women, Brought Us a Message from China," *Knoxville Sentinel*, January 31, 1920, 24.
79. *Knoxville Journal*, October 21, 1936, 16.
80. *Knoxville Journal and Tribune*, October 1, 1913, 10.
81. "Thomas W. Keller (obituary)," *Knoxville Sentinel*, March 16, 1916, 12.
82. "Katherine Bishir," NC Architects & Builders: A Biographical Dictionary, 2018, www.ncarchitects.lib.ncsu.edu.
83. *Knoxville Sentinel*, April 23, 1907, 2.
84. *Knoxville Sentinel*, September 18, 1907, 9.
85. William MacArthur Jr., *Knoxville: Crossroads of the New South* (Tulsa, OK: Continental Heritage Press, 1982), 20–3.
86. Mary Rothrock, *The French Broad-Holston Country: A History of Knox County, TN* (Knoxville: East Tennessee Historical Society, 1972).
87. *Knoxville Register*, March 16, 1819, 3.
88. Reverend P.D. Cowan, "When Knoxville Was the Capitol: Some Early History of the City and Section," *Knoxville Sentinel*, November 28, 1908, 2.
89. "Removed from Kentucky to Tennessee Cemetery: Remains of Col. Charles McClung Buried at Harrodsburg Over Sixty Years Ago," *Paducah (KY) News-Democrat*, December 20, 1904, 2.
90. *Knoxville Journal*, May 19, 1943, 5.
91. *Knoxville Journal*, September 21, 1952, 13.
92. "Local Girl Makes Good," *Knoxville Journal*, July 16, 1933, 19.
93. "The Parnassus Club," Columbia University, 2001, www.columbia.edu.
94. "Miss Mary F. Merwin (obituary)," *Brooklyn Daily Eagle*, May 17, 1941, 9.
95. "Stupendous Amusement Program," *Knoxville Journal*, September 15, 1927, 7.
96. "…then *you* write it…and she did," *Knoxville News-Sentinel*, November 16, 1960, 3.
97. Jack Neely, "National Cemetery Part II," Knoxville History Project, www.knoxvillehistoryproject.org.

98. Rule, *Standard History of Knoxville, Tennessee*, 583.

99. "Mrs. Richardson Is Dead: Created Custom that Became National," *Boston Globe*, February 10, 1911, 8.

100. "She Originated National Custom," *Berkshire (MA) Eagle*, February 10, 1911, 3.

101. "Mary and Librarian Debate It," *Knoxville Journal*, August 24, 1930, 15.

102. Mary Mallory, "The Rare Vision of Mary Utopia Rothrock: Organizing Regional Library Services in the Tennessee Valley," *Library Quarterly* 65, no. 1 (1995): 62–88.

103. Hendrik Willem Van Loon, *The Story of Mankind* (New York: H. Liveright Publisher, 1921), 7.

104. Elizabeth H. Thigpen, "Mary Utopia Rothrock: The Radical Librarian; A Historical Case Study of One Librarian's Influence as a Librarian, Educator, and Historian" (Dissertation, Robert Gordon University, Aberdeen Business School, Department of Information Management).

105. "Gen. Schubert Dead: Remarkable Career of a Young Man Who Came to Knoxville Penniless—His Great Big Heart" (obituary), *Knoxville Journal and Tribune*, June 4, 1895, 5,

106. Bonnie L. Gamble, "Nashville and Chattanooga Railroad," Tennessee Encyclopedia, Tennessee Historical Society, 2017, www.tennesseeencyclopedia.net.

107. "Machinists' Lodge Charter Member Holds Record Tenure as Treasurer," *Knoxville Journal*, January 26, 1950, 10.

108. Jeff Davis, "Amtrak at 50: The Rail Passenger Service Act of 1970," ENO Center for Transportation, October 30, 2020.

109. "Southern 154—1890 Schenectady Locomotive Works," Three Rivers Rambler, www.threeriversrambler.com.

110. Thomas H. Johnson, ed., *Emily Dickinson, Selected Letters* (Cambridge, MA: Belknap Press of Harvard University, 1958).

111. *A History and Biographical Cyclopaedia of Butler County, Ohio, with Illustrations and Sketches of Its Representative Men and Pioneers* (Cincinnati, OH: Western Biographical Publishing Company, 1882).

112. William Rule, "Death of Colonel Edward Maynard," *Brownlow's Knoxville (TN) Whig*, February 19, 1868, 2.

113. *Knoxville (TN) Daily Chronicle*, November 6, 1880, 1.

114. *Brownlow's Knoxville Whig*, February 12, 1868, 2.

115. *Journal and Tribune*, October 6, 1923, 5.

116. Betsey Creekmore, "Catherine Wiley," Volopedia, University of Tennessee Libraries, 2018, https://volumes.lib.utk.edu/news/volopedia-encyclopedia-of-ut-history-and-traditions-now-online.

117. *Nashville (TN) Banner*, March 14, 1903, 10.

118. *Knoxville (TN) Daily Tribune*, March 29, 1883, 1.

119. *Daily Press and Herald*, June 10, 1875, 4.

120. John C. Ewers, "The Influence of Epidemics on the Indian Populations and Cultures of Texas," *Plains Anthropologist* 18, no. 60 (May 1973): 104–15.

121. Vernie A. Stembridge, "Herff, Ferdinand Ludwig (1820–1912)," Texas State Historical Association, 1952, updated 2019.

122. Matt Lakin, *Knox News* (Knoxville, TN), January 29, 2012.

123. "Charles Coburn,» Turner Classic Movies, www.tcm.com.

124. "Summer School of the South," *University of Tennessee Register*, 1915–16, 84.

125. Ivah died on April 27, 1937, and according to the April 29, 1937 *Knoxville Journal*, she had, shortly before, "written Miss Della Yoe of 1643 White avenue, an intimate friend and associate, that she was homesick for the South and wanted again to see the Smokies."

126. *Knoxville News-Sentinel*, February 25, 1916, 6.

127. "Emancipated Women Set Up Hobby-Houses in Adamless Eden Back in Wilds of Smokies," *Knoxville Journal*, October 27, 1935, 1.

128. *Knoxville Journal*, July 3, 1932, 15.

129. "For the Boys Over There," 1918 United War Work Campaign, www.unitedwarwork.com.

130. Lucy Templeton, *Knoxville News-Sentinel*, September 8, 1926.

131. Betsey B. Creekmore, Volopedia, University of Tennessee Libraries, https://volumes.lib.utk.edu/news/volopedia-encyclopedia-of-ut-history-and-traditions-now-online.

SOURCES

Digital Library of Tennessee. "Views in Lida (McClung) Ross's Garden." https://tntel.info/resource/digital-library-tennessee.

Find a Grave. www.findagrave.com.

Knoxville Journal. "Funeral Rites Today for Ross, Industrialist." November 29, 1956, 1, 2.

Knoxville News Sentinel archives, 1922–90.

———. "William Cary Ross, Business Leader, Dies." November 28, 1956, 1, 2.

McClung Digital Collection of the East Tennessee Historical Center. Knoxville, Tennessee.

Neely, Jack. Articles in *Metropulse* (Knoxville, TN) and *Knoxville (TN) Mercury*.

———. "Secret Gardens: The Wildest Prettiest Places Just under Knoxville's Nose." *Metropulse* (Knoxville, TN), March 3, 2000.

New York Times digital archives.

———. "Ihigene Ochs Sulzberger Is Dead: Central Figure in Times History." February 2, 1927.

Rule, William. *Standard History of Knoxville, Tennessee, with Full Outline of the Natural Advantages, Early Settlement, Territorial Government, Indian Troubles and General and Particular History of the City Down to the Present Time*. Chicago: Lewis Publishing Company, 1900.

Talese, Gay. *The Kingdom and the Power: Behind the Scenes at The* New York Times*: The Institution that Influences the World*. New York: World Publishing Company, 1969.

Wikipedia. "History of Fort Sanders, Knoxville, Tennessee." www.wikipedia.org.

ABOUT THE AUTHOR

J udy Loest was born in Snowflake, Virginia, and has lived in Knoxville, Tennessee, for forty years. She holds a master's degree in English from the University of Tennessee, is the editor of *Knoxville Bound: A Collection of Literary Works Inspired by Knoxville, Tennessee* and is a member of the Old Gray Cemetery Board of Trustees.

Visit us at
www.historypress.com